HAMILTON EAST PUBLIC LIBRARY
W9-BST-262
5 0508 01960 882 8

658.872 Fiu 2011
Fiumara, Georganne.
How to start a home-based mail order business 6/11

9780762763641

how to start a home-based

Mail Order Business

HOME-BASED BUSINESS SERIES

how to start a home-based

Mail Order Business

Fourth Edition

Georganne Fiumara

gpp®
Guilford, Connecticut

Hamilton East Public Library
One Library Plaza
Noblesville, IN 46060

With love for my husband, Glen, my partner in mail order . . . and in life, and for my children, Brett and Marissa, my reasons for starting a home-based mail order business

To buy books in quantity for corporate use
or incentives, call **(800) 962-0973**
or e-mail **premiums@GlobePequot.com.**

Copyright © 1996, 2000, 2005, 2011 by Georganne Fiumara
Fourth Edition Printing 2011

ALL RIGHTS RESERVED. No part of this book may be reproduced or transmitted in any form by any means, electronic or mechanical, including photocopying and recording, or by any information storage and retrieval system, except as may be expressly permitted in writing from the publisher. Requests for permission should be addressed to Globe Pequot Press, Attn: Rights and Permissions Department, P.O. Box 480, Guilford, CT 06437.

Editorial Director: Cynthia Hughes
Editor: Katie Benoit
Project Editor: Tracee Williams
Text Design: Sheryl P. Kober
Layout: Kevin Mak

Reprint permission for promotional materials that appear on p. 59 granted by Phyllis Cox.

ISSN 1550-6592
ISBN 978-0-7627-6364-1

Printed in the United States of America
10 9 8 7 6 5 4 3 2 1

This book's purpose is to provide accurate and authoritative information on the topics covered. It is sold with the understanding that neither the author nor the publisher is engaged in rendering legal, financial, accounting, and other professional services. Neither Globe Pequot Press nor the author assumes any liability resulting from action taken based on the information included herein. Mention of a company name does not constitute endorsement.

Contents

Acknowledgments

Writing a book is never a singular pursuit.

This one would not have been written if not for:

Jan Melnik, thanks for the recommendation . . .

Mike Urban, Elizabeth Taylor, and Katie Benoit at Globe Pequot Press . . .

And, of course, the fans of HomeWorkingMom.com: I appreciate the way you've shared your hearts and your businesses with me throughout the years . . .

And my family, for always supporting my work at home.

Introduction

It was a dark and rainy November afternoon. I was one of a long line of dripping-wet people waiting in line at the post office. To help pass the time I began reading the posters decorating the walls. My eyes fell on a handwritten sign that read: POST OFFICE BOXES AVAILABLE. As an aspiring mail order business owner, this bit of information interested me, for I had always heard that it was difficult to obtain a post office box. When my turn finally came, I casually inquired about the fee. "Twenty dollars per year," said the postal clerk. Without taking time to think, I replied, "I'll take one."

On that day in 1983, I had no idea what I was going to do with that post office box, nor did I realize that renting one was my first official step toward owning and operating a home-based mail order business. For the next year, I tried out a few business ideas and learned from my mistakes. I'm not sure that I would have begun that process without that empty, waiting post office box as my incentive.

I was an aspiring writer then, with only two published pieces. I decided to write informational booklets, publish them myself, and sell them via mail order. My first booklet, titled *Mothers' Money-Making Manual*, was written to teach mothers that they could work at home—an ignored work option at that time.

Because I was working at home with two small children, I searched for affordable ways to promote my booklet by mail order. My need for market research was minimal because I was a member of my own target audience! I needed to reach young mothers who wanted to work at home so that they could take care of their children. I realized that most mothers at that time had never considered using home business as a way to solve their mothering and work dilemma. I thought, "How can I make the work-at-home option better known?" I decided to start an organization to help mothers who choose to work at home.

After developing a business plan, I wrote a press release and mailed it to all the women's magazines and newspapers across the country, announcing the formation of Mothers' Home Business Network. The press release was mailed on a Thursday, and on the following Monday my telephone began to ring. *The Detroit Free Press, Working Mother* magazine, *Baby Talk, American Baby* . . . it was just the beginning of media attention that continues today. The information about Mothers' Home Business Network appeared first in the *Detroit Free Press.* Before long, MHBN had 30 members—and every one of them was from Detroit!

Impressed by my press release, some of these magazines asked me to write articles for mothers who wanted to work at home. I developed a newsletter that I called *Homeworking Mothers* and made my original booklet a membership benefit. Two years later, *Family Circle* asked me to write a series of ten articles titled "Careers At Home." Since then I have devoted my career to writing about home business topics.

If an inexperienced young mother living on Long Island can create a national organization and become a home business expert—all via mail order—then you can find success in your mailbox too. When I started, the only equipment I had was an electronic typewriter. I kept records on file cards and paid for typesetting when my newsletter was published. Today, I can create, manage, and transmit information around the world in seconds, right from my own home office. What a difference just a few years can make!

You are starting your home-based mail order business in the midst of this wonderful revolution, with advantages that I did not have when I started. But technology won't ensure your success. You need the right information, some business sense, and a good idea to help you create a desirable product, plus a great marketing plan. A high-tech home office will enhance your creativity and raise your home business to a level not possible a few years ago. Because mail order means that you are delivering a product from a remote location, just about every website selling a product or service qualifies as a mail order business. This is the most important way technology has opened the horizons of mail order entrepreneurs. The best part is that it is not as complicated or as expensive as you might think.

Since that fateful day in the post office, more than 500,000 letters have been delivered to P.O. Box 423, East Meadow, NY 11554. And many more visit my website at www.HomeWorkingMom.com! I learned about the mail order business the hard way—through trial and error and extensive research. It is my pleasure to share everything I know with you in the pages of this book. If you'd like to share your thoughts or experiences with me along the way, I'd love to hear from you. Live links to the references and resources made in the pages of this book can be accessed on the companion website located at: www.HomeWorkingMom.com/for-readers-of-how-to-start-a-home-based-mail-order-business. We will make future updates to the book available on this site. You will also find an e-mail link that you can use to reach me directly.

01 The Magic of Mail Order

If you have always dreamed of starting a home-based mail order business, you have chosen the right book. Today is the day your dream begins to come true. Everything you need to know is contained in these pages. Take my hand, and I will guide you from start-up to success and beyond. All you have to do is add your own creativity and before you know it, you will have joined a long line of successful home-based mail order entrepreneurs.

Staying at home and making money in your own mail order business certainly seems like a magical opportunity. If you stop to think about it, you will realize that even the most amazing magic tricks are made possible by the behind-the-scenes knowledge and careful planning of the magician. If he depended on luck or deviated from his plan, his trick would fail. Poor planning can affect a new mail order business, just as it can affect a magician's performance.

Mail order is not one specific type of business but a precise marketing method. Any business involving the remote exchange of a product or service for payment can be considered a mail order business. Whether you use the mail, telephone, website, fax, print, radio, or television to promote your business and receive orders, delivery will almost always be accomplished via mail or digital delivery online. This lack of face-to-face contact makes mail order especially appealing to home-based business owners. Opening and operating a home-based mail order business eliminates the need for a storefront or a rented office, so your start-up costs are reduced. The local businessperson's sales depend on neighborhood traffic and ads in the daily newspaper. When you sell by mail or online, your reach for potential customers extends across the country and around the world.

Mail Order Today

Mail order has survived and thrived throughout the years for two reasons: roots and wings. The roots are being supplied by traditional direct marketing principles. These principles have prevailed, because they help ensure the highest possible response. Those who learn and use these rules to test their ideas actually face very little risk. Technological advances are helping to supply the wings for the mail order industry. Society has changed, and the mail order industry has responded. Both men and women work and have little time for shopping, but these busy people still want instant gratification. Today, customers can place orders online or by telephone. Overnight delivery puts purchases in the hands of very grateful customers the very next day.

You will find everything you need to know about the new and the tried-and-true mail order methods right in this book. I promise that your journey down the pathway to success will be fun and painless. Before we begin, let's see how much you already know about starting a mail order business.

How Much Do You Know about Mail Order?

1. Starting a mail order business is as easy as picking a product, putting an ad in a magazine, and waiting for the orders. **T or F**
2. You need to invest at least $10,000 to start a mail order business. **T or F**
3. You can't run a mail order business without a computer. **T or F**
4. You need a large office and lots of storage space to run a mail order business at home. **T or F**
5. To sell the most products, catalogs should offer a wide array of merchandise. **T or F**
6. The best mailing list is one you can rent from a successful company. **T or F**
7. To get started, you should always advertise in the publication with the largest circulation and the lowest advertising rate. **T or F**
8. A successful mail order business can be built with one great product. **T or F**
9. One person working at home cannot compete with the megamarketing methods of major corporations. **T or F**

Mail Order Myths

If you realize that the answer to each of the quiz questions is "False," you already know a lot about mail order. But don't worry. If you got them all wrong and all you know is that you want to work at home, and mail order seems like a good idea, you will be an expert in the time it takes to read this book.

Let's take a look at the answers to these questions as well as some other common mail order myths.

Quiz Answers

1. Many people lose a great deal of money each year because they do not realize that an interesting product alone is usually not enough to entice people to buy. When new mail order entrepreneurs spend thousands of dollars on advertising and expect that will be enough to attract customers, they are making a big mistake. In other words, don't spend $1,000 on an ad and then sit back and wait for the orders to pour in. They almost never do.
2. There is no set amount of money needed to start a mail order business. Although it is true that undercapitalization is one reason businesses fail, lack of information can be more deadly. Money will power your ideas and help you reach your goals, but information will give you the power to spend your money in the correct ways. If you are strapped for cash, don't despair. I will show you how to get started on a shoestring.
3. Years ago many a mail order business was started and run without a computer. File cards contained the all-important customer names, addresses, and buying history, and master sheets of names and addresses were photocopied onto labels so that mailings could be done. No, I am not recommending that you start a mail order business without a computer. Today, computers have become the heart of even the smallest home-based operation; however, if you are waiting to start your business because you don't have a computer or don't know how to use one, you are making a mistake. Start to work your business and keep track of your customer information in the best way you can develop. I'll show you how to incorporate computer technology into your business.
4. It would be great to have a large office and lots of storage space for your home-based mail order business. If you are living in a studio apartment, does that mean you can't fulfill your dream? No way. There are ways to set up your business in the smallest of spaces and use outside resources to help you. Stay tuned, and I'll show you how.

5. Specialization has become an essential element to mail order success. A wide array of products is fine, but only if they appeal to a common theme. Unrelated items will attract little attention.
6. The best mailing list is not the one you rent from a successful company. The mailing list that will pull in the greatest response will be your "house" list. That is the list of people who contact you directly to request information about your product or service.
7. Large-circulation publications will only bring you the response you desire if the publication is directed to your clearly defined target audience, no matter how reasonable their advertising rates. To be effective, advertising should be repeated on a regular basis.
8. A successful mail order business can be started with one great product, but you will not be able to sustain success unless you can offer other related products and services to your customers.
9. One person, working at home, can compete with the megamarketing methods used by large corporations. You can—and should—imitate what they do but on a smaller scale. Affordable and available technology has leveled the playing field and put the ball in your hands.

The Greatest Myth of All

Would you like to make a million dollars? Who wouldn't? Want to work at home and collect a mailbox full of checks each day? You bet. Unfortunately, this simplistic view of mail order has sold millions of books and caused many aspiring home business owners to be disappointed. There is a lot of money to be made in mail order, but you probably won't see much of it if money is your only goal.

Even though there are no quick and easy ways to develop a mail order business, there are specific, proven success formulas that you can use to create your own kind of magic. Mail order profits are a by-product of a well-planned, carefully grown mail order business. So don't look for a magic wand. Research and careful planning will help you start out right and stay in business. You can make money in mail order and even achieve magical results, but first you must take the time to learn the tricks of the trade.

Common Mail Order Start-Up Questions

Q: Is it really possible to start a successful mail order business from my home?

A: Sure, it is possible to really make it big when starting at home. Many major corporations had home business beginnings. Hallmark Cards, Lillian Vernon, Apple Computer, even Domino's Pizza, were started at home.

Q: Isn't a home-based mail order business kind of old-fashioned?

A: Not at all! Technology has made it possible to attract even more business! The checks in your mailbox are now supplemented by orders that arrive via telephone or Internet. The mail order industry has embraced the technological changes. And even in the twenty-first century, products ordered still must be sent to the customer by mail or a delivery service. Any transaction that does not take place in person can be considered mail order.

Q: I'm not sure that I want to work at home. Should I wait until I can rent an outside space before I start my mail order business?

A: Starting a business from home allows you to eliminate many expenses such as rent, commuting, and utilities. This will enhance your chances of success and allow you to start your business with less cash. Why wait? You can always move your business out of your home after it has been established.

02 Managing Mail Order at Home

Between the walls of your home and under one roof, many exciting possibilities exist for living and managing a mail order business. When you work at home, you can become anything you want to be, and you don't need anyone's permission to begin. Living and working in the same place can be a dream come true or a nightmare that never ends. The way you feel will be determined by your basic personality and the amount of planning you do. In this chapter, you will learn about the pleasures and perils of working at home—the real story. You'll find out about all of the possible problems and how to avoid them. Then we'll design an office that will fit in your home and fill it with the right equipment to help you run your mail order business. But first answer the following questions to find out if you have a personality suitable for working at home.

Will You Be Happy Working at Home?

1. *Do you like to make plans and do research?* This is a wonderful time to be starting a home business. Libraries and bookstores are filled with books on every aspect of small-business ownership, and there are so many role models to emulate. The Internet offers an unending source of free information. Reading this book is a wonderful starting point, but you will have to continue doing research and plan every step of your business if you want to succeed. You will find all the help you need in the appendix.
2. *Are you a self-starter?* It has been called the two-minute commute, but getting there is just the beginning when you work at home. As a

home business owner, you will have to have the discipline to plan your day and work your plan even though no one is watching.

3. *Are you a decision maker?* Do you like being in charge? Do you have the courage of your convictions? As a home business owner you need to make decisions every day. Unless you have self-confidence, the smallest dilemma could cause problems.
4. *Are you flexible?* You must be decisive, but you also need to change your mind as situations arise. Flexibility is required when your personal life interferes with your business. You might have to stop and start your projects throughout the day to handle family obligations, or make up for lost time by working at night.
5. *Do you know your limitations?* When you own your own business, you won't be able to do everything yourself. You may be helpless with numbers or lack writing talent. If you can recognize your weak points and find others to do those jobs for you, your chances of success will improve.
6. *Can you live without a weekly paycheck?* When you own a home-based business, your income depends on your hard work and a little luck. That means that there is no limit on the amount of money you can earn. But if you can only be happy when you know exactly how much income you will make each week, the roller-coaster ride of business ownership may not be for you.
7. *Will you respect your business?* If you don't feel like you are really working when you are tending to your home business, neither will your family and friends. It is up to you to respect your work time, so that others won't impose their needs or interrupt for unimportant reasons.
8. *Can you set goals?* You have to know where you are going before you can find the right pathway. Long-term and short-term goals are an important part of business planning.
9. *Are you creative?* Creative thinking is vital when you are starting a business. Ideas will fuel your ambitions and help you see situations from every angle. Starting a business is as creative as painting a masterpiece or writing a novel.
10. *Are you persistent?* You must be willing to hear "no" in order to hear "yes." Everyone encounters negative reactions. Some people cannot take rejection and stop trying, but those who keep trying will be the only ones who eventually succeed. Only you can limit your chances for success.

Don't worry if you cannot answer "yes" to every one of these questions. You can develop some of these qualities and find others to help you manage.

If, however, you answered "no" to most of the questions, you might want to rethink your business plans.

Making the Most of Working at Home

Managing time and fighting isolation are two challenges that new home business owners face. If you make plans now, you can avoid having problems later. As you design your perfect work-at-home lifestyle, be sure to factor in time for work and family, and time for interacting with others in business.

Managing Your Time

When you work at home, it doesn't take long to get to work, but it can take forever to get your work done if you allow yourself to be constantly interrupted and distracted by outside influences. You don't have to enter your home office at 9:00 a.m. and work until 5:00 p.m. That would be unrealistic and eliminate part of the charm of working at home. But even though you probably won't have a traditional workday, you should establish a schedule that fits into your life and follow it as closely as possible.

While my children were little, I often went to work when my husband arrived home. Although some work was done during daylight hours, my workday started at about 7:00 p.m. and usually continued until 2:00 or 3:00 a.m. An eight-hour workday is an eight-hour workday—no matter which eight hours you work. I grew to like those hours that gave me a silent house and the ability to concentrate on the job at hand. You might prefer to go to bed early and wake up at 5:00 a.m. to get your work done. Don't be afraid to do what works for you, but do it consistently.

Here are a few time management tips to help you squeeze every minute out of your day:

- *Leave 20 percent of your day unscheduled.* Leaving open time will help you to adapt easily to any emergencies that may arise and help you finish those projects currently in progress. Even if you have to accomplish a large number of tasks, do not plan to do too much in one day. You will be setting yourself up for feelings of frustration, and you will feel out of control.

- *Use the telephone and e-mail.* Telephone calls, texting, and e-mail can save a great deal of time and energy. If you place calls before 9:00 a.m. or after 4:30 p.m., your chances of reaching the person you are calling will be enhanced. When leaving a message, state a specific time when you can be reached, and provide enough information so that the person will be prepared to speak with you when the call is returned. E-mail can be an even more effective way to exchange information and get a timely response. Those who will not return phone calls often respond to e-mail. If you can establish a text message relationship, all the better!
- *Set goals.* All of us have dreams and wishes, but goals are specific, measurable, and realistic statements of intent. Although few people would get into their cars without a destination in mind, many try to run their lives and their businesses without well-defined goals. This spontaneous and flexible approach to home business can easily let you roam far off course before you even realize how much time, energy, and effort you have wasted. To be most effective, write down short-term, midterm, and long-term goals, and create a measurable, step-by-step plan for achieving them. Then at the end of each workday, write a to-do list for the following day, keeping your goals in mind.
- *Learn to say "no."* If you take on more responsibilities than you can manage comfortably, your work and family life will suffer. When a project is presented ask yourself two questions: (1) Will doing this increase my knowledge or my income? (2) Will the benefit to my family be worthwhile? If you cannot answer "yes" to one of these questions, smile sweetly and say "no."
- *Delegate.* Home business owners get into trouble when they try to handle every aspect of their business by themselves. Establish a network of people to help you accomplish tasks that are not the best use of your time. You may give up some control, but you will gain the time you need to do more important work.

Avoiding Isolation

Those who work at home expect to spend many hours alone. Some miss the daily interaction with coworkers; others prefer the solitary lifestyle. Even though your neighbors and non-business associates offer friendship, and your family will support you emotionally, only others in your field can give you the kind of feedback that will be useful in your business. It is also important to keep in touch with new developments in your field, and locate resources to use when you are in need of help. Best of all, interaction with business colleagues can boost your creative energy, which is the power that will help your home-based mail order business grow and prosper.

It is possible to reap the rewards of interacting with colleagues without sacrificing your independence.

Here are some easy ways to avoid feeling isolated:

- *Network by telephone and e-mail.* I've never met my most valuable business associates. My list of contacts is endless, as is the help and encouragement I receive from these people. Chances are we will never have a face-to-face meeting, but that's okay with me. I'm used to being on a first-name basis with other writers, editors, publishers, publicity representatives, home business owners, virtual assistants, and others I have come to know well through our letters, e-mails, and telephone calls. Successful networking relationships such as these evolve because each of us has something to contribute to the relationship.
- *Network in person.* You can join a formal networking group, such as your local chamber of commerce or a home-based business organization that meets on a regular basis. Once you meet others who share your interests, you can start a smaller, more informal group to discuss issues and brainstorm ideas.
- *Monitor the media.* When an important news event happens, the country and sometimes the entire world stops to watch. Keep track of current events by watching the news and reading the newspaper each day. You will find interesting tidbits of information that could help you promote your business, and you will maintain a connection with the world around you.

Homeworking Harmony

Parenting and running a home business offer separate and satisfying rewards. There are many who would say it is virtually impossible to work while taking care of children. I am here to tell you that not only is it possible, it can be preferable. I and thousands—maybe millions—of other parents work while caring for our children every day. In fact, parents have always cleaned the house or done one sort of job or another with children around. However, there is a downside to working at home with children that you should anticipate. If you are prepared, you may be able to avoid some of the common pitfalls.

One day in particular stands out in my mind, a day that began calmly and then brought me troubles in pairs. My daughter, Marissa, then age six, and my son, Brett, who was eleven at the time, woke up with the flu. Because their rooms are located on opposite sides of the house, and their throats were too sore to call out to me, I gave each a bell to ring. Their stereo chiming served as background music throughout a day that took no heed of my two impending deadlines, two telephones ringing (more bells!), and two important appointments that had to be postponed.

That was a difficult day, but the number two eventually proved lucky. Marissa and Brett recovered from the flu just two short days after receiving the type of care only a parent could give. If my business had been located outside my home, chances are that my routine would have been disrupted anyway, and my children would have had a stranger soothing their fevers and nursing them back to health.

My kids are independent (and healthy) adults now, and I have worked at home during my entire parenting experience. Believe it or not, children can actually benefit from growing up in a homeworking family.

Children who are exposed daily to the sights and sounds of business absorb a great deal of what they see and hear. The opportunity to learn every aspect of business during childhood is a rare gift that many children begin to appreciate at an early age. The availability of computers, fax machines, and other high-tech equipment in many home offices gives these kids an advantage that other children do not have.

The age of your child will determine the best techniques for parenting while working. Consider the following age-appropriate tips:

- *Newborn to age two*—Kids this age need constant supervision, so you have to work while they are sleeping, watching television, or playing in the same room as you, or while they are with another caretaker. Try placing a baby seat near your desk, and talk or sing as you work for short periods of time. A backpack or front baby sling can work well when a baby is under six months old. One mother reported typing so often while she was pregnant that when she put her baby in a backpack, the sound of her keyboard lulled the baby to sleep.

If you can hire help, choose someone who can work in the business or care for your child, as needed. Even if you only work part-time at this stage, it is beneficial for your child to see you working. Seeing you work and speak on the telephone each day will pave the way for his or her acceptance of your business in the years to come.

- *Ages three to five*—Schedule work periods during the same time each day, and be sure to follow with a child-centered activity. A toy telephone, typewriter or computer, and art supplies will keep your children occupied at their own miniature desk, which you can put next to yours. Save discarded mail for cutting and pasting. You'd be surprised how much time you can buy with a roll of tape and some colored paper. Give your little ones actual "jobs" to do each day, such as turning on the computer and pasting stamps on envelopes and mailing them. While keeping your children busy and happy, you are also giving them an opportunity to learn and contribute to your business a little at a time.
- *Ages six to ten*—School age! Now you have about six hours of uninterrupted time each day. Don't waste it doing housework or errands. If you work during this time, you will not have to steal much time away from your kids when they are at home or need rides to after-school activities. This is the time to involve your children in your business. Explain what you are doing, and share your plans. Ask them for help, and pay them for the work they do. When your business has some success, share it with them by going out to eat at their favorite restaurant to celebrate.
- *Ages eleven to eighteen*—All the rules change when your children reach double digits. Not only do they not want your attention all the time, they will probably wish that you worked in an office outside your home. But this is the age that they need your supervision the most. The older the child, the more necessary it is to have after-school supervision. The ways they can get in trouble multiply. Being available to discuss problems and oversee homework right after school improves communication. Older children can be a real help with your business and may appreciate having the opportunity to earn extra money right in their own homes; however, loud stereos and other disturbances during business hours can be hard to bear. And kids in this age range may even resent having too much business-related activity going on around them.

To avoid problems, I have devised a list of ten rules for homeworking families that will promote harmony between the generations:

Rules for Parents

1. *Keep home business papers, supplies, and equipment out of family areas.* The products of a home business will inevitably take over the whole house if we allow that to happen. This can be especially upsetting to a child who is trying to eat at a kitchen table filled with work or entertain friends in a living room decorated with boxes or mailbags.
2. *Create standard working hours when possible.* When you work at home, it is easy to work too much. Try to work within a schedule, taking full advantage of school hours and the time the children are sleeping. Whenever possible, stop work at a time they can count on each day.
3. *Set fair limits.* Don't expect the house to be quiet all of the time. Rules and regulations during regular business hours are okay, but the kids should know that they can let loose when work time is over.
4. *Don't require kids to work.* It's great to have an opportunity to earn extra money, but don't make children do a job that they don't want to do. If there is an emergency, and you need their help, explain the situation. If they don't volunteer to help, make other arrangements, and don't count on them in the future.
5. *Provide tangible benefits.* Pay the going rate for any work your kids do. Try to make time for them to use your computer or other equipment. Once in a while, just take the afternoon off and do something special together—something a parent who works outside the home cannot do.

Rules for Kids

1. *Appreciate the reasons why your parents are working at home.* It is likely that one of the reasons the home-based business was started was so that your parents would have more time to spend with you. When there is a lot of work to do, it may seem like they don't have any time for you at all. They were there for you when you were small, and they are still there when you need them now.

2. *Respect the business.* At least part of your family's income is dependent on the success of the business. If there is a business call, make sure that there are no loud noises in the house while your parent is speaking. Maintain a positive attitude, and don't make your parents feel guilty when they have to work.
3. *Don't take your parents for granted.* If you need a ride or want a parent to participate in a school function, don't just assume that it will be possible. Even though they are working at home, sometimes it's not possible to drop everything. You are lucky enough to have at least one parent available to you when others don't, and if you try to make your needs known in advance, they can be scheduled into the day.
4. *Take advantage of the home office.* Learn about your parent's computer and other office equipment. If you need extra money, be happy that the business provides a convenient way to earn the extra cash you need.
5. *Keep your promises.* If you promise to work, be ready on time, and work as seriously as you would for any other job. If you promise to use headphones to listen to music during business hours, do it without being reminded. Explain your parent's business to your friends so that they will follow the rules too.

Designing Your Home Office

Not long ago, home businesses were referred to as "kitchen table enterprises." Those who worked at home dreamed of making a lot of money, but most did not generate enough income to warrant a separate home office or even a desk and chair. Work was done at the kitchen or dining room table after the dinner dishes were cleared. When the home business world went high-tech, everything changed. Overnight, home business owners could afford to own the same equipment used by major corporations, which made them serious competitors in the marketplace. The home business was taken out of the kitchen and into specially designed work spaces.

Whether you live in a tiny apartment or a spacious house, you must consider your particular needs before you start planning your work space. To create a home office that suits you and your business, you need more than a desk and chair in the corner of the den. A well-planned home office should be appealing, functional, and located as far away from family living quarters as possible. Separation is necessary so that noise and interruptions won't disrupt work, and work won't interfere with the business of living. No one wants to feel as though they live in an office, and that kind of atmosphere is particularly unfair to other family members. You will have particular needs that only you can determine, so here are some questions to ask yourself:

1. Will you work during daytime hours or will you be burning the midnight oil?
2. Will family members be at home during your work hours?
3. Do you want to be accessible to young children, or are you eager to be shut off from the rest of the family?
4. Will you be making and receiving important telephone calls?
5. How much equipment and furniture will you be purchasing?
6. Will you have to entertain clients in your office?

Home-based office space can be found in very unexpected places. A spare bedroom is an obvious choice, but if you don't have an entire room available to you, try to think creatively. You can carve out a work area from limited surroundings. An alcove, the space under a stairway, a breakfast nook, and a large closet are some spaces to consider. Or you might set up your furniture and equipment along one straight wall and screen it with a freestanding room divider or bookcase.

Do you have a little-used dining room or garage? As long as family members agree, you can change the previously designated use of a room. There is one benefit to taking space from a part of your home that is now being used for something else. You will be making a statement to yourself and your family: Your business is important and deserves special consideration.

Don't choose a dingy, dark basement, a hot attic, or a closed-in but cold front porch unless you are willing to make the changes necessary to transform your space. Ignoring creature comforts is a mistake. You will spend a lot of time in your office, and you don't want to dread going to work. You want to create a pleasant environment that reflects your personality, your priorities, your family's needs, and the amount of space and money you have available. Add heat, air-conditioning, or a dehumidifier, paint the walls a bright color, and use extra lighting for dark spaces. A few plants under plant lights can help make up for a lack of windows.

Remember, you will always need more space than you anticipate. More than one home business owner has reported moving a home office from space to space within the home as the business expanded. You will save yourself a lot of trouble if you allow as much space as possible from the start.

If there is absolutely no space available in your home to set up an office, it is possible to purchase a specially designed cabinet that will open up to reveal shelves, filing cabinets, and work surfaces. When you are finished working, the whole system can be folded up. A wide variety of foldaway home offices is available in office and furniture stores as well as catalogs.

Making It Yours

Once you determine the best space available, it is time to select your furniture and the other items that will transform the area into a real office. A comfortable chair, work surface, computer furniture, bookcases, and filing cabinets come first. Then get the decorations and other niceties that create a welcoming atmosphere. When you are in the start-up phase of a business, your home office needs to be comfortable and functional. Don't make the mistake of spending all your start-up money on your office, leaving little for marketing and product development. You can always update your furniture as your business grows. In the beginning, spend your money on marketing that will attract customers and on equipment that will empower you to meet your goals.

Most home business owners agree that your chair is the most important piece of furniture you will buy, so it should be purchased first. An uncomfortable chair is not only unpleasant, but it also can be unhealthy. Your back, knees, and circulation could be put in jeopardy if you use the wrong chair. A good chair will be adjustable, the back will support you with adequate padding, and the front part of the seat should "cascade" or bend toward the floor. This will prevent the circulation in your legs from being cut off. The only way to choose a chair is to try it out, but be ready to pay. A good chair will cost at least $250.

Once you have an adjustable and comfortable chair, you can buy all other items gradually. If you make sure that your work surface and keyboard holder are the correct height in relation to your chair height, your desk and computer table do not have to be fancy or even new.

It is also important to have a separate telephone line installed right in your office space to use for your business only. When the business telephone rings, you will know for sure that it is a business call. This will allow you always to answer calls in a professional manner—in person or by answering machine or voice mail. Make sure that the telephone you choose also has a "hold" button on it so that you can put a conversation on hold if you need to quiet down background voices or noise.

Businesses can also benefit by having a business telephone line, because such a connection makes you eligible to place an ad in the Yellow Pages, and your number will be listed in "Information" under your business name when potential customers want to call.

One final note: Check the electrical outlets in your planned work space, and make sure you have enough electricity to power your computer and other equipment. How your computer will get online? If you are using a laptop, you may have Wi-Fi or use a router to your main computer. You can also use a cable or telephone modem or a DSL connection.

Mail Order Work Space

When you run a home-based mail order business, you will have specific equipment needs. Because you will be opening letters, sorting mail, stuffing envelopes, and fulfilling orders, you will need a long table. If you have the space, set up a permanent worktable. You might consider buying file cabinets or other low storage cabinets of the same height and placing one or more unfinished doors on top of the cabinets. Leave room between the cabinets for foot space. If space is a problem, purchase a folding table that is at least 6 feet long.

Next you need an area to store your promotional materials and the products that you sell. Your storage system will also depend on the amount of space you have available. A large office with a permanently assembled table can use open bookcases for product storage and a tabletop organizer with slots to fit letter (8½-by-11-inch) pieces of paper. If space is a problem, you could put shelves in a closet or buy a freestanding closet that can be closed at the end of the workday. If you are selling products that take up a lot of space, or if you have large boxes of printed material to store, you may have to consider renting a garage or a storage space outside of your home. But be careful when storing paper: A dank or humid atmosphere could affect the paper's weight and appearance. Never put boxes of printed materials directly on the floor of a garage, because water or other liquid could seep through.

Your Computer and Other Equipment Needs

With a flick of a switch you can be ready to manage your customer list, track inventory, create professional documents, do accounting, designing, writing, planning, access a world of information, and much more.

The most difficult part of computerizing your home office is choosing the right computer for your needs. Don't panic. You didn't have to become a mechanical genius before you selected your last car or an electronics expert prior to purchasing your television. Learning what you need in a new computer or how to upgrade the one you already have can be managed in the same way.

Before you even begin to look at computers, look at the programs or software that make them run. Look at the mailing list programs, the word processing programs, the graphics programs. Many programs are available on CD-ROM. Look over the titles and if you are interested in them, make sure you have a built-in CD-ROM drive in your computer. Each program lists the minimum requirements for running the program on a computer. While you are doing your research, you will find that the amount of RAM (Random Access Memory) and the size of the hard disk drive will be the most important considerations when trying to run software. Think of RAM as the amount of intelligence a computer has and the hard disk drive as the amount of space a computer has to store the software applications you choose and the subsequent work you do with them. When you know what kind of programs you want to run, you will begin to know what kind of computer to buy.

To complete your research, begin to read computer books and magazines aimed toward the new user. (Computer software and reference materials are listed in the appendix of this book.) Then, visit personal computer shows and stores. Try to choose stores where the sales personnel are not paid on commission, so you will not feel pressured to buy. Discuss your needs with more than one salesperson and compare their recommendations. As your knowledge increases, everything will start to make more sense, and you will begin to have a preference for one computer over the others.

Here are some factors to consider as you make your decision:

1. *What is your budget?*
2. *Do you know someone whom you can consult on computer matters?* Do you have business colleagues with whom you must share information? If so, what type of computer do they use?
3. *Is ease of use your most important consideration?* If so, you should probably give serious consideration to Apple Macintosh computers—my first and only choice. Apple's iMac computer is geared to new users and is powerful enough for any home business. Affordably priced, it comes Internet-ready.

More Working Wonders

The best way to select the right equipment for your home office is to make a list of the tasks you need to do frequently and then find the equipment that will expedite your work. It is a mistake to purchase equipment or services that you anticipate needing. The need must exist first; however, having a need is still not enough reason to buy. There is a more important reason to delay purchases, beyond the expense factor. Advances in technology come quickly. As time passes, the equipment available becomes more advanced and the price becomes more affordable.

Here are some choices you might consider for your home-based mail order business:

Multi-Function Printer

A multi-function printer is a computer printer, scanner, and photocopier all in one unit. This is a cost-effective and space-saving way to get the technology you need. Before you decide which model is best for you, be realistic about the jobs you need to do and the ways you will use your printer. Do you really need a wireless connection? If not, the price of your unit will go down dramatically. Will you be printing photos or need color copies? If not, a black ink only printer will reduce your investment to below $200.

Fax Machine or Fax Software

E-mail has replaced many of the ways businesses were using faxes, but there are many ways the fax machine is still a valuable resource. If you need to send a contract with a signature, forms with blanks filled in, or documents with handwritten corrections, e-mail will not work. Besides basic faxing, you can do fax broadcasting, which will send a scanned document to a selected group of recipients automatically, or fax-on-demand, which will allow your customers to request printed information and receive it by fax—all without your direct assistance. Since these types of fax services can be costly, consider using a service bureau to handle them.

Automatic Back-up

Don't wait for your computer hard drive to crash, taking all the information on your computer along with it. Yes, it can happen to you. It happened to me—twice—before I got smart. The first time, the technician was able to restore much of my information. The second time, I lost everything. My iMac has a feature called Time Machine. I attached an inexpensive hard drive to my computer and it now automatically copies everything on my internal hard drive. If I click on the external hard drive, I can see that it is really a complete copy, with nothing to restore and no technical worries. If you do not have a Macintosh computer with Time Machine, you could manually drag your important information to an external hard drive each night or pay for online backup that you won't have to think about.

Telephone with Voice Mail and Headset

Your telephone should have all of today's basic features available, such as call waiting and call forwarding. If you expect to make long distance calls, get a calling plan that gives you unlimited long distance for one monthly fee. You will probably need to use your computer while you speak on the phone, so get a headset that will free your hands to work as you speak. A cordless headset will give you full access to your office while you are on the phone.

Cell Phone

As a home business owner, you have the freedom to come and go as you please. But that doesn't mean that business stops when you are out of the office. Some home business owners use a cell phone as their business line, but it is preferable to have a landline in your office that will forward your business calls to your cell phone when you are out of the office. Your phone can be as simple or as feature-rich as you need. Again, the word "need" is important when you chose your cell phone. Do you really need to go online and have "apps" that count your calories or give you games to play on your phone? Do you feel the need to tweet every move you make? Or, do you just need basic communication and a keyboard for easy texting? Choose carefully because monthly charges could skyrocket if your use your phone as a mini-computer.

Digital Camera

If you are going to put your products on eBay or need to take photos to put on your website, a good digital camera with at least ten megapixels is essential. Photos to be used online don't need to be high-resolution, but there are some features that are important to look for. You want your camera to have macro ability so that you can take close-up photos of practically anything. Be sure that your camera can connect to your computer. You can get a lot of camera for a very reasonable price, so do your homework and learn about the different models before you go shopping. You can also ask friends how they like their cameras and ask if you can take a photo to see how it feels.

Common Mail Order Managing Questions

Q: How many hours per week will I need to devote to running my mail order business?

A: In the start-up phase, you will spend as much time as possible planning and creating your mail order business. Once your ideas take hold and you begin to receive orders, you will have to work as long as it takes to fill those orders and generate new ones. As your business grows, so will the time you need to dedicate to it. If you have chosen a concept that excites you, every minute you can dedicate to your business will be fulfilling, even if you are working more hours for less money than ever before. If you put in the time, you will eventually profit from the experience.

Q: Do I need a college degree before I can start my mail order business?

A: No. I have done home business consulting for people with marketing degrees and years of experience in the corporate world. They often ask me how to find customers for their new home businesses, even though they did just that on a corporate level. Yes, you need information—good, solid, home business information—before you can begin. All of the information you need is contained in books like this one. Add your own creativity, common sense, and a network of other business owners, and you will not need a college degree to create a successful mail order business.

Q: I'm afraid my children will feel rejected if I work at home. There will be times when I won't be able to respond to their needs immediately or will have to close them out of my office. What do other parents do?

A: If you have young children and work that cannot be started and stopped throughout the day, you will need to have someone to help you with child care. If, however, your children are old enough to function on their own for at least part of the day, they will benefit from the supervised independence they will have while you are working at home. They will feel as though they are managing themselves, but you can keep an ear and one eye on them just in case of a problem. If you make rules before any trouble starts and try to work during the same hours each day, your children will consider your business part of their lifestyle. Explain why you are closing your door, and let them know that they can open it in an emergency. Communication and planning will help you create the atmosphere you are seeking.

03 Perfectly Painless Business Planning

Do terms such as "cash flow," "taxes," and "business plan" make you feel uneasy? The decisions that must be made and the steps that must be taken at the very beginning of a home business can be so confusing and overwhelming that many people never progress beyond the starting point. Are you stopped cold by questions such as the following: Do I need to register my business name? How do I declare my business at tax time? What kinds of records must I keep? If so, don't worry. In this chapter, you will learn everything you need to get your mail order business started using my perfectly painless planning system. You bought this book because you want to start a mail order business, so I will emphasize the fun things such as choosing the right products and selecting a great name. When it comes to your business structure and the financial aspects, I will take the basic and easy approach. In the start-up phase of a home-based mail order business, complicated record keeping is not necessary.

Business Ideas Are All Around You

What came first, the chicken or the egg? Should you choose a product first and then find a market, or should you target a market and create a needed product? Actually either method can be successful. The most important point to remember is that you cannot develop your business without considering both the items to be sold and the customers who would be interested in what you have to offer.

You can begin with just one product, experiment with it, and learn all you can about the people who purchase it. Then you must gradually add more products and services to sell to those who bought your lead product.

There has been a lot of research done on choosing a product or service that can be successfully sold via mail order. Before you can begin to evaluate your ideas using the guidelines I will give you, you have to have an idea worth considering.

Ideas are all around you. In order to find the right one, you need to stop, look, and listen.

Stop Waiting for Perfection

Ideas evolve and tend to take on a life of their own once you set them free. Time must pass before you will know for sure if you are heading in the right direction. You will experience a few false starts and decide more than once that you will not continue in a direction that had seemed correct at the start. You have to give yourself permission to stumble and make mistakes, for only the people who are willing to risk failure will have earned the opportunity to succeed.

Look within Yourself and All around You

Finding the right business idea is a process that requires you to look deep within yourself to discover your talents. Only then can you begin to evaluate all of the potential mail order ideas you encounter each day. To help you decide, buy an idea notebook and a file box to keep your source material in one place. Write down every idea or inspiration you have in your idea book. Look at your hobbies and interests, the clubs you belong to, the jobs you have held. Don't consider selling a product that is unrelated to any of your real-life experiences.

Research the products that interest you by reading about them and speaking with people who are selling or using them. If possible, work part-time or volunteer your help in a business selling similar goods to get an insider's view. Careful research will help you develop a support system of references and people who can give you the insight you need as your business progresses.

Ideas and appealing products are all around you. Successful mail order entrepreneurs realize that there are very few original ideas. The most successful companies often take an idea that is already working for someone else, improve or change it, and make it their own.

Listen to Your Heart

Once you have found the right product or service to offer, don't let anyone or anything stop you from pursuing it.

Evaluating a Product

Products and services that will sell via mail order need to have the following attributes in common. To make it easy, just keep the letter **U** in mind.

Unique—Everyone wants to feel special. Owning a product that is off the beaten path can contribute to that feeling.

Useful—Customers buy because they feel that their purchase will solve or prevent a problem.

Unavailable—If the product you choose is widely available in stores, it will be more difficult to convince your customer to buy through the mail. Choose a product that is unavailable in stores, or give an alternate reason why they should buy from you, such as a low price or fast delivery.

Understandable—The product you choose should have benefits that can easily be conveyed to the customer. If they don't understand what you are offering, they won't bother to investigate the benefits.

Used up—If possible, choose items that get consumed, requiring another purchase.

Universal appeal—This is the one **U** word that you do *not* want your product to match. It is impossible to find a product that appeals to everyone. If you try to please everyone, you will please no one.

Unconscious desires—People place orders thinking that they have a need for a product. But in reality, buying decisions are often based on an individual's emotional response.

Unlimited profits will be yours if you choose products that will help your customers feel secure, popular, healthy, attractive, clean, stylish, creative, self-confident, successful, or just plain happy. If you can help them save time, escape pain, make money, influence others, satisfy curiosity, or avoid trouble, the dollars will fill your bank account.

In addition to these attributes, your product should be easy to mail and readily available from suppliers or your own production.

Locating Suppliers

Okay, you know what you want to sell. Now who will supply your product? Everything from baby wipes to crafts have been produced by entrepreneurs in their homes and sold by mail order. Printed materials such as newsletters or "how-to" booklets that you produce yourself are always a good choice. You can rely on your own expertise and a local printer to obtain your product. If, however, you must purchase your product from a wholesale source, it can get more complicated.

Here are some of the best methods for finding a supplier for your chosen product.

- *Look in your mailbox.* Send away for catalogs and informational materials from companies that operate within your area of interest. If you see a product you'd like to sell, contact the manufacturer directly.
- *Go to the library.* Look for *Thomas's Register of American Manufacturers* (or online, www.thomasregister.com) and the Catalog of Catalogs (Woodbine House). Check the *Business-to-Business Yellow Pages* for large cities across the country.
- *Read trade publications.* There are newspapers and magazines dedicated to the interests of most industries. They will help you get an insider's view.
- *Attend trade shows.* Trade shows in your area of interest will be advertised in the trade publications you read. Try to determine the products receiving the most interest. Collect printed information given out by the manufacturers. If possible, have your business card available before you attend to give to companies that interest you.
- *Go shopping.* If you find a product that interests you, check the manufacturer's tag and contact the company.

Important note: In most states, before you will be permitted to buy products for wholesale prices, you will have to have a resale tax certificate. It may have a different name in your state, but the reason for obtaining this certificate is clear. It permits you to purchase your merchandise without paying state sales tax. You will then be required to collect sales tax from the final user of the product. You are not required to collect tax from sales going to states other than the one in which you are located. Consult your state's sales tax office for further details. Beyond a resale certificate, most manufacturers will also require that you purchase minimum quantities of a product, and some will not sell to you unless you have a storefront. When contacting a manufacturer, use business stationery to make a professional impression.

Pricing Your Product

There are three factors you need to consider when determining a price for your product:

1. *How much will you spend on advertising and postage?* This figure must include any paid advertising and the cost of printing your promotional materials. The postage figure comes from the amount of postage for your direct-mail efforts.
2. *What is the wholesale cost of your product?* Be sure to include the cost of having the products shipped to you, and your packaging and shipping costs when you make a sale. To simplify your analysis, take your wholesale cost and multiply it by four. This will probably cover your expenses and allow you to make a profit. Does the total sound like an appropriate price? If you are accepting credit card orders, make an allowance for the fees involved.
3. *What price will your target market ultimately be willing to pay?* What price is being charged for similar merchandise? If your figure seems low, don't be afraid to increase it. You will encounter many hidden costs. And if the price is too low, your potential customer may not feel that quality merchandise is being offered. There is an implied value in a higher price; however, make sure your price is market-driven. If you raise your prices and your market is unwilling or unable to pay the higher price and your competition has lower prices, your price increase will not be accepted.

The Name Game

Choosing a name for your mail order business is one of the most important decisions you will make. Your choice will have a big impact on the public's perception of your business and ultimately on your success. To help you decide on the best name, you can play The Name Game. If you take the time to learn the rules of the game, you will know how to give your business the winning edge it deserves.

The Object of the Game

To win The Name Game, you must create a business name that lets your potential customer know exactly what type of product or service your business is offering in as few words as possible. The grand prize (maximum sales) will go to the business name that also allows for any future shift in the direction of the business and communicates the benefits your customer will receive.

Strategy

Keep Your Options Open

To be a winner, your home business name must encompass the products you sell now, as well as any new products or services your company might offer in the future. Suppose you are selling handcrafted toy trains. You might consider calling your business Tom's Toy Trains. Bad choice. Naming the business "Tom's" tells the public that this is probably a one-person operation. "Toy Trains" limits the kind of wooden creations you could make. Instead, you could follow the lead of Connie and Timothy Long of Questa, New Mexico. This husband and wife named their handmade wooden toy business North Star Toys—not Tim and Connie's Wooden Toys. The name North Star Toys evokes a magical image that subtly reminds customers of Christmas and keeps their options open to sell any kind of plaything. A perfect name.

Know Your Business, Know Your Customer

When you are naming your business, it is particularly important to choose a name that is descriptive and conveys professionalism. You wouldn't want potential customers to think that your products or services are produced with less concern and care than in a business located outside the home.

Even though you are just getting started, you must have a clear picture of your business now and a plan for the future before you can choose a name. What products or services will your business provide, and who will your customers be? Once you know your target audience, you will be able to select a name that appeals to that particular type of person. For each business name you consider, try to envision how your customers will perceive your business, what they will expect from you, and how that name will convince them that you can fill their needs. When chosen with your customer in mind, your business name should be able to instill confidence.

Winning Move: Getting It "Write"

Use a pencil and paper to make your most important move. Without being too critical, write down all of the words that are associated with your business, including those words that will give your customers the impression that you will be able to meet their needs. When you have a page full of these words, begin to place some of them together and see how they sound. You might even coin a new word by combining two words into one. As you go through this process, keep your potential customer in mind.

Next write a list of your competitors' business names. Determine which ones are most effective and why. Eliminate the words that are too close to a competitor's name from your list. How do the names you are considering compare to the best names of similar businesses? Take note of other business names you encounter, and write down the ones you like and dislike, and then ask yourself why. This will help you use the qualities of the best names and avoid making the same mistakes others have made.

More Do's and Don'ts to Consider

1. *Don't* pick a name that is too long, confusing, or hard to pronounce.
2. *Don't* choose a name that another business is already using in your local area or on a national level.
3. *Do* choose a name that appeals not only to you but also to the type of person you are trying to attract as a customer.
4. *Don't* select a name that relies on a cute pun that amuses you but does not make sense to your potential customer.
5. *Don't* use the word "Enterprises" after your name, because it is often used by amateurs. And be sure you don't use "Inc." if your company is not incorporated.
6. *Do* choose a name that is familiar or comforting. If you can conjure up a pleasant memory, potential customers might respond to your business on an emotional level.
7. *Do* choose a name that can also be used as a domain name for your website.

A Second Chance to Win

If you have already played The Name Game and lost, you can give your business a second chance to win. You don't have to live with a name that is too vague, too cute, or did not allow for the change of direction that your business has taken. You can alter your business name gradually by combining the new name with the old to give your customers enough time to adjust.

Here is an example:

Original name:	Michael's Muffins
First change:	Michael's Marvelous Muffins

After a while:	Drop "Michael's," add "and More"
The result:	Marvelous Muffins and More

The new name is more descriptive and leaves room for future expansion of the business.

Bonus Point: Give Your Name a Graphic Image

Shakespeare wrote, "What's in a name? That which we call a rose by any other name would smell as sweet." But no one would ever smell a rose if it was called "stinky" and looked like a weed. An appropriate and appealing name can help you project the right image only if you represent that name with an eye-catching logo and promotional pieces.

Most business owners would not go to an important business meeting in a sweatshirt and torn jeans; however, many do use hastily rubber-stamped envelopes or poorly photocopied flyers with crooked type. Your printed materials will represent your business at thousands of one-on-one business meetings each year and should make a great impression while serving as effective communication tools. Even the most brilliantly written copy will go unread if the package is unappealing. The recipient will think that the business has invested little thought or care in creating its image, and the whole mess will end up in the trash.

New mail order business owners should never skimp on printed materials. Unless you have artistic ability and can produce impressive results, it is wise to consult a professional artist for help in developing a graphic image. These services can be expensive but will pay dividends in the months and years to come. An artist will develop your logo, which will symbolically depict your business name, and design your brochure, stationery, and business cards

Choose an artist who will not impose his or her vision on you but will breathe life into your ideas and concepts. Ask to see a portfolio of logos, letterheads, and brochures the artist has designed for previous clients, and don't be afraid to interview more than one person. Some additional considerations: Get price quotes up front, ask to see rough layouts before final designs are done, and ask about the amount of time needed to complete your project. The artist can help you choose paper and select a typeface, but once the artwork is finished, it belongs to you. Take possession of the original artwork from the artist after your materials have been printed. This will give you greater control and allow you to choose a different printer next time.

Be sure to register your business name with your county clerk. It can be utterly heartbreaking—and expensive—if your logo has been designed and your brochure and stationery have already been printed, and you find out that someone else is already using your name.

A Great Defense

To protect your company's new name and logo, you should consider a trademark. Before finalizing your name, do a trademark search, using a trademark attorney, or if you have a large library available to you, look in the annual edition of *Trademark Register of the U.S.* Online computer searches are also possible. Consult your librarian for help.

It is possible to file a trademark up to three years before actually using it. As soon as you begin to put your name into use, you can put a little ™ next to it, even though it has not been registered. This will deter others from using it and act as an announcement that you may be in the process of filing a trademark. Use of the trademark symbol does not obligate you to file a trademark.

Beyond your trademark, be sure to protect your company's name online. Whether you have a website now or not, you should register your business name in every form it might take. If someone could add an "s" and register a name very much like yours, you should register it first. The cost of registering a domain name can be very affordable now and should not stop you from taking this important step.

A Winning Combination

To attract your customers, your mail order business needs the best business name, represented by appealing and effective promotional tools. That winning combination will help you develop a successful home business and leave you smiling . . . and smelling like a rose.

Setting Up Your Business

Business Structure

There are four basic forms of business ownership. Once you understand each option, you should have no trouble selecting the one that is right for you.

Sole Proprietorship. The majority of home businesses are formed as sole proprietorships, because it is the easiest business structure to start and the most simple to terminate. A sole proprietor has total control of all business assets and is responsible for all debts incurred by the business. Taxes are paid as part of the owner's personal tax return by filing a form called Schedule C.

Partnership. Many people feel more comfortable starting a business with a partner, but think carefully before choosing this business structure. In a business partnership, partners can make business decisions without the other's approval, but debts and liability extend to all partners. In other words, your personal assets can be seized if your business partner makes a costly mistake. A legal partnership agreement is strongly advised to clarify each partner's role, but even this will not protect you financially. If you choose to become a partner, choose your associate with great care.

Corporation. Although this is the most complicated business structure to form, it also provides the most personal protection. Simply put, a corporation is a group of people who form a separate legal entity that can operate as one body. The owners, or shareholders, risk only the money they invest. They cannot be held personally responsible for the debts or liabilities of the business unless they sign a separate personal guarantee with a lender. Corporations are required to keep more detailed records, and the help of an attorney is usually required. This form of ownership is usually not recommended for new home business owners unless the business presents unusual liability.

LLC or Limited Liability Company. This business structure gives the owner limited liability protection with more flexibility in tax and management structure than a corporation. Available in the majority of states and a large number of foreign countries, an LLC protects its members from personal liability for paying the debts of the company. If there is more than one member of an LLC, they can choose to be taxed as a partnership. A single member can pay taxes like a sole proprietor. An LLC can be formed by filing a certificate of formation with your state. Fill-in the blanks forms are usually available for this purpose.

Business Licenses and Registration

Once you have named your business and have chosen the type of business structure that is right for you, you are ready to register your business. A telephone call to your city or county clerk will help to clarify the requirements on a local level. You may or may not need a business license, depending on your type of business. In general, if you are operating a food-related business or another type of business that can affect the health or well-being of the public, you will have to obtain permits and licenses.

If you are using a business name that is different from your own name, it is likely that you will have to file a "fictitious name" statement or obtain a "DBA" (doing business as) certificate. Again, your city or county clerk will be able to tell you about local requirements. Most banks will not open a business checking account in your business name unless you have one of these certificates. Because it is important to have such a checking account, it is necessary to complete this step.

Mail Delivery

Where will you receive your mail? It is not a good idea to use your home address. You want your home business to maintain a low profile (see Zoning Considerations below) in your neighborhood. Even if you don't anticipate receiving a lot of mail, that can change. A large sack full of letters (containing checks?) will thrill you, but the person who delivers your mail will not be happy. Using your home address also makes it possible for your customers to come to your door without warning.

Renting a box at your local post office or at a storefront mailbox center is your best option. There are pros and cons to each. The cost per box is much higher at a mailbox store, but they offer some services you cannot get at the post office. Most provide a call-in service that allows you to find out if you have mail. If you will be shipping and receiving large boxes, mailbox stores will send and receive UPS shipments for you. They will also provide a street address that can inspire confidence (box numbers are listed as suite numbers). However, I recommend using a post office box, simply because it will cost less and there is little danger of the post office closing. Mailbox stores can go out of business, and if that happens, you will have to change your address.

Know Thy Neighbor—Zoning Considerations

If you can stand outside your home and not be able to tell that you have a home business, you probably do not have to worry about zoning problems. Because yours is a mail order operation, you will not have customers visiting your house. You will not create any unusual smells, unpleasant noises, or any other hazard or nuisance. If your mail is delivered to a post office box and you don't have large trucks making frequent deliveries, your neighbors won't know about your business unless you tell them.

Every state except Vermont allows local municipalities to determine zoning regulations. You can make a call to your county clerk to learn the restrictions in your area so that you will be protected if any of your neighbors decide to complain. If an irate neighbor turns you in, you will have few options beyond applying for a special-use permit or a variance. So be careful that you do not threaten the residential nature of your neighborhood.

Credit Card Merchant Account

You cannot run a mail order business unless you can accept credit cards. Until recently, banks have discriminated against home-based businesses of all types and especially those that operate via mail order. Because an increasing number of businesses are being started at home, some of these banks are realizing that they should take another look at their policies. In other words, they want your business, but they don't want risky business.

Thankfully, your local bank is no longer the only source of merchant status. American Express and Discover Card are non-bank companies that are slightly more lenient than banks. If you apply to them first and are accepted, you could develop a track record that would impress the bankcard companies. Visa and MasterCard are available only through banks, independent sales organizations (ISOs), or a merchant credit card processor.

If you live in a rural area, you will have less trouble establishing a merchant account with your local bank. Banks in urban areas usually have tougher standards. No matter where you live, try your local banks first. If you have your business checking account in the bank and have significant deposits, it might help you receive a positive decision.

If your local banks turn you down, try an ISO. ISOs act as intermediaries between small businesses and banks. Although it is very important for a mail order business to be able to accept credit card purchases, if you are not careful, you could lose money. Pay special attention to application fees, sales percentages, and the cost of leasing or purchasing equipment. These and monthly fees can vary widely. Don't jump at your first acceptance. Shop around for the best deal, and factor in these fees when you set your prices. For more information about getting a merchant account, see Profit Profile: Merchant Warehouse (page 147).

Your Business Plans—Two for the Money

There are two types of business plans: formal and informal. You will need a formal business plan for the purpose of getting a loan or attracting potential financial investors. It is a very structured (and often intimidating) document. During the start-up phase of business, many owners fear writing a formal business plan. If you share that feeling, don't worry. If you are not ready or able to supply the needed details for a formal business plan, you probably don't need one yet.

An informal business plan is one you write yourself, for your eyes only. It is a living document that can be changed as you learn from experience and as your business grows. Every business owner needs an informal business plan. The good news is that once you have completed all the steps in this chapter, you will have most of the information you need to write your informal business plan.

In keeping with our simple and easy theme, I am going to give you an overview of writing a formal business plan and include some hints for obtaining a bank loan. Then we will return to the comfort zone and begin writing your informal business plan and explore some of the more creative methods for financing your dream.

Formal Business Plan

Unless and until you are trying to obtain a bank loan or other financing, it is not necessary to write a formal business plan. Writing a formal plan can help you focus on the amount of money you need to run the business and to examine each detail with the eye of a banker. But if you do not feel ready to deal with the information in this section, just skip it for now and go directly to working on your informal plan.

Your formal business plan must be well written, look professional, and be able to keep the attention of a banker who may not want to spend much time with it. The person evaluating your plan wants to see evidence that your company is focused, that there is something special or unique about your business, that you have the ability to make your company a success, and that you have a proven record of attracting customers. Most importantly, you need to prove that there will be a return on the investment.

When you write your plan, do not put too much emphasis on your company's product or service. Instead, write about your target market, what it needs, and how your company will fill that need. If you are serious about obtaining financing, it is a good idea to get professional help when preparing your business plan. Check the appendix for some resources that can assist you.

To familiarize you with the requirements for writing a formal business plan, here are the essential components that must be present.

1. *Cover Page.* Include your company's name, address, telephone number, and your name. If you have a logo, put in on the cover page for a professional appearance.
2. *Table of Contents.* Each page should be numbered, and each section should be titled. Do the table of contents last.
3. *Executive Summary.* This is the most important part of your business plan, because it will be read first; if it is not convincing, the reader will not continue. The executive summary must be a dynamic introduction and description of your company. You must summarize the most important points of each section of your plan in just two or three pages. Write the executive summary after you have completed the main part of your plan.
4. *Company Description and History.* Here you will describe the origin of the company, your objectives, and how you arrived at this point.
5. *Product or Service Description.* What makes your product or service more appealing than your competition's? How is it made, and why is this a good time to expand your operation?
6. *Marketing Plan.* Describe your target market, including detailed demographics. Why will these customers buy your product? What price will they be willing to pay, and how will you make a profit? What is your sales strategy?
7. *Operational Plan.* How will you acquire or produce the product you sell? How is it manufactured? How will you deliver it? Can you protect your concept?
8. *Management Team.* People are more important than products or anything else to those contemplating financial involvement in your business. You must demonstrate your credentials and how others will enhance your operation. Unfortunately, most banks and other investors want to see a management team, not an individual. If you do not work with anyone else yet, describe who you will hire after you get the money you are seeking.
9. *Financial Plan.* This is not the place for unsubstantiated guessing. Your sales projections, cost estimates, past and projected cash flow statements, income statements, and balance sheets must be based on known facts or the results of careful research. Experts say that most people involved in reading business plans will not take your figures at face value. It is likely that they will believe half of your sales projections and double your anticipated expenses.

10. *Support Documents.* Your sales materials are listed here, including ads and press releases, photographs, résumés of key personnel, letters of intent, and market surveys. All of these materials and more can add support to your written plan.
11. *Presentation.* The entire business plan should be laser printed on white paper and put in a binding that will allow it to lie flat when opened. Make sure that you proofread for mistakes.
12. *Cover Letter.* A personal letter addressed to the person who will be reviewing your business plan is definitely a must. It should explain why you are submitting the plan to that person. Point out a key point in the plan that you think will be of particular interest to the recipient, and direct him or her to that exact page.

Important Notes on Bank Loans

Convincing a bank to give you a loan is a lot like making a sale to one of your customers. You need to understand the needs and motivations of both. The loan officer's main concern is that the money lent to you will be repaid. To qualify for a loan, you have to set yourself apart from the crowd and convey the feeling that you are prepared and professional. Simply put, the banker wants to know how much money you are requesting, what you are going to do with it, how your business will benefit, when and how you will pay it back, and what happens if you don't. You will not receive a loan until you can provide the answers to all of these questions.

If you are seeking a loan of $100,000 or less, there is some good news. The Small Business Administration (SBA) has made it a lot easier. The SBA does not make loans, but they can guarantee the business loans that are made by your local banker, which reduces the risk to the bank. SBA loan guarantees are available to existing small businesses, not new ones. The SBA has reduced its thick application to just one page. As a result, the SBA is granting twice as many loan guarantees as before. For more information on this program or to receive start-up assistance, you can either call (800) 8-ASK-SBA or go to the SBA website at www.sba.gov.

Informal Business Plan

Your home-based mail order business needs a plan. Writing down your plans will help you remain focused. You can start your informal planning simply by writing one very short paragraph. If you are focused, you should be able to summarize the purpose of your business in just a few sentences. Then you need to address how your business will operate, the financial aspects, and your marketing plan.

We've already discussed many of your operating concerns in this chapter, and you can use the upcoming checklist to make sure that you've addressed all the important issues. Because marketing is the heart of your business (and so much more fun than the other stuff), I have devoted an entire chapter to it. You will learn all about creating a marketing plan in chapter 5. That leaves your financial planning.

Easy Financial Planning

At the beginning of this chapter, I promised to keep the financial aspects of business planning simple. It is very unlikely that you will make a profit your first year in business. That doesn't mean that you won't have money to spend. It means that your qualified business expenses will offset your gross business income. It is important to keep records, but if you are like most new business owners, you resist record keeping. This is a mistake. The amount of money coming in and going out of your business is a barometer of your success. And it helps you answer many important questions: Does your income show that you are making the right moves? Are your expenses too high? Will you have enough money to proceed with your plans in the future? Will you have the information you need to prepare your tax return?

As you can see, keeping track of your cash is important, but it does not have to be complicated, especially during the start-up phase of your home-based mail order business. My start-up method requires only three simple things: a business checking account, a large monthly wall calendar, and a monthly accordion file.

Business Checking Account. This is your first and most important step on the road to easy record keeping. All of your business money will be deposited in this account, and all of your business-related expenses will be paid from this account. Each time you make a deposit or write a check, you will make a clear notation of where each deposit came from and why each check was written.

Large Monthly Wall Calendar. Use your large monthly wall calendar to quickly note the day's income and expenses, and the total at the end of each week. One look at your calendar page will give you a good overview of the month's activity. Besides noting your income and expenses, indicate the days your mailings have been sent or advertisements have appeared. Then note the number of inquiries received as a result of these marketing efforts. This will give you a quick impression of the response you are receiving to each of your marketing efforts. Make sure your calendar is large, and use a different color ink for each type of entry so that you will be able to distinguish each bit of information at a glance.

Monthly Accordion File. Every time you make a purchase, file the receipt in your monthly accordion file. Note the check number on each receipt.

These easy-to-do records will provide enough information for your personal use and will allow you to file accurate tax returns. If you eventually need to create more formal financial documents, these records will provide the information you need to proceed.

How Much Money Do You Need?

During your first year in business, you will need to purchase everything from a computer to paper clips. How much money will you need to finance your home-based mail order business? One mail order book I read suggests that you will need about $400 to get started—the cost of one advertisement and some sales materials. This is a gross underestimate. Even if you are selling a service instead of a product, your minimum start-up costs will be higher than you anticipate. It is more difficult to start a business with limited capital, but it can be done.

The amount of money needed to open and operate your home-based mail order business depends on the kinds of products or services you will be selling. However, there are expenses that all new mail order home business owners share.

The forms on the next two pages will help you anticipate how much money you need when your investment is low (page 39) and what you can add if you have enough start-up cash (page 40).

Financing Your Dream

If you have a marketable product or service, a basic understanding of small business principles, and a lot of common sense, you can begin to work on your business right now, even if you do not have a lot of investment capital. Once you begin, you will realize that money is only one of the tools you need to start a successful mail order business. Possibilities make us all rich. Because you are starting your business at home, you can explore all of these possibilities without spending a great deal of money. A low-budget business start-up means that you begin gradually, and all income goes back into the business. It also means that you must use your creativity and initiative instead of cash to help your business grow.

When I started my home-based mail order business, personal computers were just becoming affordable and available. I used index cards to keep records, typed master sheets to photocopy onto labels when I did mailings, paid to have my brochure and newsletter typeset, and used my electronic typewriter to write articles and letters. I operated like that for four years. Because my investment was small, I had the time and flexibility I needed to make mistakes. Had I made a large

Expense Summary

Lower-Investment Start-up

Market research	$__________
Product development	__________
Inventory of products	__________
Business licenses and permits	__________
Insurance (consult your agent)	__________
Bank fees	__________
Merchant fees for credit cards	__________
Telephone deposit	__________
Brochures	__________
Business cards	__________
Envelopes	__________
Labels	__________
Other sales materials	__________
Mailing-list rentals	__________
Packing materials	__________
Postage	__________
Product shipping costs	__________
Initial advertising and public relations	__________
Trade books and publication subscriptions	__________
Office supplies	__________
Operating capital	__________
TOTAL	$__________

investment, I would have been pressured to make a profit without delay, and I might have made some foolish moves.

The sad truth is that a bank is more likely to grant a loan for home improvements or a vacation before they grant one for business start-up, especially if you have not already invested some of your own cash. Why should others offer to invest their money if you are unwilling to risk your savings? Many aspiring business owners take

Expense Summary

Higher-Investment Start-up

Computer	$__________
Computer software	__________
Computer training	__________
Printer	__________
Modem	__________
Online service charges	__________
Desk	__________
Ergonomic chair	__________
Computer table	__________
Product storage shelves	__________
Worktable	__________
Postage machine	__________
Copier	__________
Fax machine	__________
Fax-dedicated telephone line	__________
Voice mail service	__________
Legal and professional fees	__________
Office remodeling	__________
Additional operating capital	__________
Other	__________
TOTAL	$__________

a second mortgage on their homes. I strongly urge you not to do that, especially at start-up. You do not want to risk your home to test a business idea.

Most new businesses are owner-financed. I financed my business by gradually investing personal funds until the business started generating some working capital. To help you figure out how much money you can spare each month for your business, fill in the appropriate figures:

Fixed Monthly Expenses + Variable Monthly Expenses
= Monthly Expenses

Net Monthly Income from All Sources – Monthly Expenses
= Discretionary Income

Your discretionary income will be the source of your business investment plus any other money you have in savings. Family and friends may want to invest in your business, but remember that you may give up some of your independence if you accept money from outside sources who may want to have control over your decisions.

Here are some ways to make a splash with little cash:

- *Get a job.* Working part-time for another mail order business can give you an insider's view of a successful operation and help you finance your own ideas.
- *Start two businesses.* Some business ideas have long-range possibilities but will not provide immediate income. If you need quick cash, a temporary alternate pursuit can help you finance your dream venture. Many aspiring home business owners work as direct sales representatives for established companies. Direct sales can help you develop sales skills. If you choose to sell products that appeal to the target audience for your mail order venture, you will have the opportunity to do some market research as you sell the products.
- *Barter.* Doctors do it. Plumbers do it. Anyone who can offer a desirable product or service can do it too. When you exchange goods or services without exchanging money, you are bartering. This is an excellent way to obtain what you need and save cash. Even though no money changes hands, the IRS wants to know about bartering arrangements, so be careful and check with your tax adviser.

- *Don't advertise . . . publicize.* The public needs to know about your business, but how can you get the word out with a small advertising budget? It is unlikely that one or two ads can produce enough response to bankroll an advertising campaign. Advertising can only be effective when it is consistently repeated. Instead of advertising, think of ways to let the maximum number of people know about your business for minimum costs. Come up with a newsworthy story about your business, and send press releases to the publications that are read by your target audience. There is more on getting publicity in chapter 5.
- *Network.* Networking has been defined as "getting together to get ahead." Joining local and national organizations will put you in touch with others who share your goals. Contacts with people who have businesses similar to yours will give you the opportunity to ask questions and learn techniques that have been successful for them. You could find many opportunities to offer and receive assistance. But remember, networking is a two-way street. Be prepared to give assistance to others as often as you receive it.

Taxing Considerations

To complete your financial planning, we need to address your tax obligations. When I file my taxes, I use a CPA, who handles my business taxes and my family's personal tax returns. I suggest that you do the same. Find a tax preparer who has special knowledge about small business filing. But even if you hire a professional, you need to have enough knowledge to ask intelligent questions. This information applies to your federal income tax. Consult your tax preparer for information on your state and local taxes.

If you are a sole proprietor, you only need to know three letters of the alphabet to know what forms are needed for your business filing: Schedule C, Profit or Loss From Business, or Schedule C-EZ, Net Profit From Business. If your business had gross receipts of $25,000 or less and business expenses of $2,500 or less, you can file Schedule C-EZ, which is a simplified form of Schedule C. These forms are filed with your regular Form 1040.

If your Schedule C shows profits of $400 or more, you must also file Schedule SE, Self-Employment Tax. Self-employment tax is a combination of Social Security and Medicare taxes.

Sample Schedule C, Profit or Loss From Business

SCHEDULE C (Form 1040)

Department of the Treasury Internal Revenue Service (99)

Profit or Loss From Business

(Sole Proprietorship)

▶ **Partnerships, joint ventures, etc., generally must file Form 1065 or 1065-B.**

▶ **Attach to Form 1040, 1040NR, or 1041.** ▶ **See Instructions for Schedule C (Form 1040).**

OMB No. 1545-0074

2010

Attachment Sequence No. **09**

Name of proprietor | **Social security number (SSN)**

A Principal business or profession, including product or service (see instructions) | **B Enter code from pages C-9, 10, & 11** ▶

C Business name. If no separate business name, leave blank. | **D Employer ID number (EIN), if any**

E Business address (including suite or room no.) ▶

City, town or post office, state, and ZIP code

F Accounting method: **(1)** ☐ Cash **(2)** ☐ Accrual **(3)** ☐ Other (specify) ▶

G Did you "materially participate" in the operation of this business during 2010? If "No," see instructions for limit on losses ☐ **Yes** ☐ **No**

H If you started or acquired this business during 2010, check here ▶ ☐

Part I Income

1	Gross receipts or sales. **Caution.** See instructions and check the box if: • This income was reported to you on Form W-2 and the "Statutory employee" box on that form was checked, or • You are a member of a qualified joint venture reporting only rental real estate income not subject to self-employment tax. Also see instructions for limit on losses. ▶ ☐	1	
2	Returns and allowances	2	
3	Subtract line 2 from line 1	3	
4	Cost of goods sold (from line 42 on page 2)	4	
5	**Gross profit.** Subtract line 4 from line 3	5	
6	Other income, including federal and state gasoline or fuel tax credit or refund (see instructions)	6	
7	**Gross income.** Add lines 5 and 6 ▶	7	

Part II Expenses. Enter expenses for business use of your home **only** on line 30.

8	Advertising	8		18	Office expense	18	
9	Car and truck expenses (see instructions)	9		19	Pension and profit-sharing plans	19	
10	Commissions and fees	10		20	Rent or lease (see instructions):		
11	Contract labor (see instructions)	11		a	Vehicles, machinery, and equipment	20a	
12	Depletion	12		b	Other business property	20b	
13	Depreciation and section 179 expense deduction (not included in Part III) (see instructions)	13		21	Repairs and maintenance	21	
				22	Supplies (not included in Part III)	22	
				23	Taxes and licenses	23	
				24	Travel, meals, and entertainment:		
				a	Travel	24a	
14	Employee benefit programs (other than on line 19)	14		b	Deductible meals and entertainment (see instructions)	24b	
15	Insurance (other than health)	15		25	Utilities	25	
16	Interest:			26	Wages (less employment credits)	26	
a	Mortgage (paid to banks, etc.)	16a		27	Other expenses (from line 48 on page 2)	27	
b	Other	16b					
17	Legal and professional services	17					

28	**Total expenses** before expenses for business use of home. Add lines 8 through 27 ▶	28	
29	Tentative profit or (loss). Subtract line 28 from line 7	29	
30	Expenses for business use of your home. Attach **Form 8829**	30	
31	**Net profit or (loss).** Subtract line 30 from line 29. • If a profit, enter on both **Form 1040, line 12,** and **Schedule SE, line 2,** or on **Form 1040NR, line 13** (if you checked the box on line 1, see instructions). Estates and trusts, enter on **Form 1041, line 3.** • If a loss, you **must** go to line 32.	31	

32 If you have a loss, check the box that describes your investment in this activity (see instructions).

• If you checked 32a, enter the loss on both **Form 1040, line 12,** and **Schedule SE, line 2,** or on **Form 1040NR, line 13** (if you checked the box on line 1, see the line 31 instructions). Estates and trusts, enter on **Form 1041, line 3.**

• If you checked 32b, you **must** attach **Form 6198.** Your loss may be limited.

32a ☐ All investment is at risk.
32b ☐ Some investment is not at risk.

For Paperwork Reduction Act Notice, see your tax return instructions. Cat. No. 11334P **Schedule C (Form 1040) 2010**

Part III **Cost of Goods Sold** (see instructions)

33 Method(s) used to value closing inventory: a ☐ Cost b ☐ Lower of cost or market c ☐ Other (attach explanation)

34 Was there any change in determining quantities, costs, or valuations between opening and closing inventory? If "Yes," attach explanation . . . ☐ **Yes** ☐ **No**

35	Inventory at beginning of year. If different from last year's closing inventory, attach explanation	35	
36	Purchases less cost of items withdrawn for personal use	36	
37	Cost of labor. Do not include any amounts paid to yourself	37	
38	Materials and supplies	38	
39	Other costs	39	
40	Add lines 35 through 39	40	
41	Inventory at end of year	41	
42	**Cost of goods sold.** Subtract line 41 from line 40. Enter the result here and on page 1, line 4	42	

Part IV **Information on Your Vehicle.** Complete this part **only** if you are claiming car or truck expenses on line 9 and are not required to file Form 4562 for this business. See the instructions for line 13 to find out if you must file Form 4562.

43 When did you place your vehicle in service for business purposes? (month, day, year) ▶ ____ / ____ / ____

44 Of the total number of miles you drove your vehicle during 2010, enter the number of miles you used your vehicle for:

a Business ____________ b Commuting (see instructions) ____________ c Other ____________

45 Was your vehicle available for personal use during off-duty hours? . . . ☐ **Yes** ☐ **No**

46 Do you (or your spouse) have another vehicle available for personal use? . . . ☐ **Yes** ☐ **No**

47a Do you have evidence to support your deduction? . . . ☐ **Yes** ☐ **No**

b If "Yes," is the evidence written? . . . ☐ **Yes** ☐ **No**

Part V **Other Expenses.** List below business expenses not included on lines 8–26 or line 30.

48 **Total other expenses.** Enter here and on page 1, line 27	48	

Sample Schedule C-EZ, Net Profit From Business

SCHEDULE C-EZ (Form 1040)

Department of the Treasury Internal Revenue Service (99)

Net Profit From Business

(Sole Proprietorship)

▶ **Partnerships, joint ventures, etc., generally must file Form 1065 or 1065-B.**
▶ **Attach to Form 1040, 1040NR, or 1041.** ▶ **See instructions on page 2.**

OMB No. 1545-0074

2010

Attachment Sequence No. **09A**

Name of proprietor | **Social security number (SSN)**

Part I **General Information**

You May Use Schedule C-EZ Instead of Schedule C Only If You:

- Had business expenses of $5,000 or less.
- Use the cash method of accounting.
- Did not have an inventory at any time during the year.
- Did not have a net loss from your business.
- Had only one business as either a sole proprietor, qualified joint venture, or statutory employee.

And You:

- Had no employees during the year.
- Are not required to file **Form 4562,** Depreciation and Amortization, for this business. See the instructions for Schedule C, line 13, to find out if you must file.
- Do not deduct expenses for business use of your home.
- Do not have prior year unallowed passive activity losses from this business.

A Principal business or profession, including product or service | **B Enter business code (see page 2)** ▶

C Business name. If no separate business name, leave blank. | **D Enter your EIN (see page 2)**

E Business address (including suite or room no.). Address not required if same as on page 1 of your tax return.

City, town or post office, state, and ZIP code

Part II **Figure Your Net Profit**

1 **Gross receipts. Caution.** See the instructions for Schedule C, line 1, and check the box if:
- This income was reported to you on Form W-2 and the "Statutory employee" box on that form was checked, or
- You are a member of a qualified joint venture reporting only rental real estate income not subject to self-employment tax.

. . . ▶ ☐ **1**

2 **Total expenses** (see page 2). If more than $5,000, you **must** use Schedule C **2**

3 **Net profit.** Subtract line 2 from line 1. If less than zero, you **must** use Schedule C. Enter on both **Form 1040, line 12,** and **Schedule SE, line 2,** or on **Form 1040NR, line 13.** (If you checked the box on line 1, **do not** report the amount from line 3 on Schedule SE, line 2.) Estates and trusts, enter on **Form 1041, line 3** **3**

Part III **Information on Your Vehicle.** Complete this part **only** if you are claiming car or truck expenses on line 2.

4 When did you place your vehicle in service for business purposes? (month, day, year) ▶ ______________.

5 Of the total number of miles you drove your vehicle during 2010, enter the number of miles you used your vehicle for:

a Business ______________ **b** Commuting (see page 2) ______________ **c** Other ______________

6 Was your vehicle available for personal use during off-duty hours? . . . . ☐ **Yes** ☐ **No**

7 Do you (or your spouse) have another vehicle available for personal use? . . . . ☐ **Yes** ☐ **No**

8a Do you have evidence to support your deduction? . . . . ☐ **Yes** ☐ **No**

b If "Yes," is the evidence written? . . . . ☐ **Yes** ☐ **No**

For Paperwork Reduction Act Notice, see your tax return instructions. Cat. No. 14374D **Schedule C-EZ (Form 1040) 2010**

SCHEDULE SE (Form 1040)

Department of the Treasury Internal Revenue Service (99)

Self-Employment Tax

▶ Attach to Form 1040 or Form 1040NR. ▶ See Instructions for Schedule SE (Form 1040).

OMB No. 1545-0074

2010

Attachment Sequence No. **17**

Name of person with **self-employment** income (as shown on Form 1040)	Social security number of person with **self-employment** income ▶

Before you begin: To determine if you must file Schedule SE, see the instructions on page SE-1.

May I Use Short Schedule SE or Must I Use Long Schedule SE?

Note. Use this flowchart **only if** you must file Schedule SE. If unsure, see *Who Must File Schedule SE* on page SE-1.

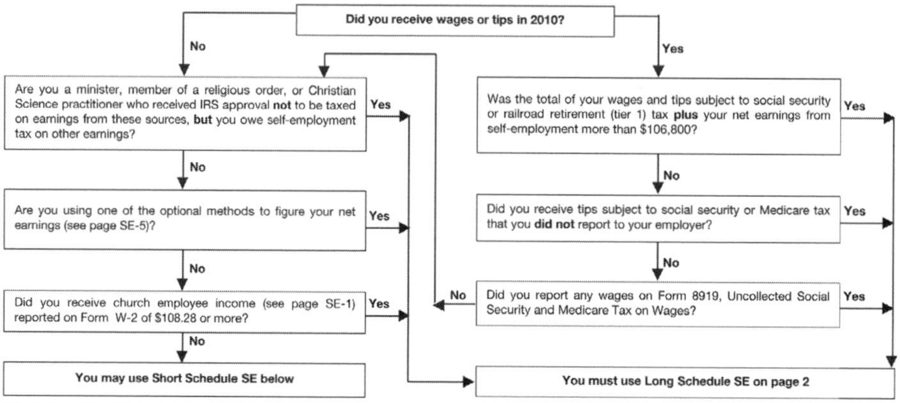

Section A—Short Schedule SE. Caution. Read above to see if you can use Short Schedule SE.

1a	Net farm profit or (loss) from Schedule F, line 36, and farm partnerships, Schedule K-1 (Form 1065), box 14, code A	**1a**	
b	If you received social security retirement or disability benefits, enter the amount of Conservation Reserve Program payments included on Schedule F, line 6b, or listed on Schedule K-1 (Form 1065), box 20, code Y	**1b**	( )
2	Net profit or (loss) from Schedule C, line 31; Schedule C-EZ, line 3; Schedule K-1 (Form 1065), box 14, code A (other than farming); and Schedule K-1 (Form 1065-B), box 9, code J1. Ministers and members of religious orders, see page SE-1 for types of income to report on this line. See page SE-3 for other income to report	**2**	
3	Combine lines 1a, 1b, and 2. Subtract from that total the amount on Form 1040, line 29, or Form 1040NR, line 29, and enter the result (see page SE-3)	**3**	
4	Multiply line 3 by 92.35% (.9235). If less than $400, you do not owe self-employment tax; **do not** file this schedule unless you have an amount on line 1b . . . . ▶	**4**	
	Note. If line 4 is less than $400 due to Conservation Reserve Program payments on line 1b, see page SE-3.		
5	**Self-employment tax.** If the amount on line 4 is: • $106,800 or less, multiply line 4 by 15.3% (.153). Enter the result here and on **Form 1040, line 56,** or **Form 1040NR, line 54** • More than $106,800, multiply line 4 by 2.9% (.029). Then, add $13,243.20 to the result. Enter the total here and on **Form 1040, line 56,** or **Form 1040NR, line 54**	**5**	
6	**Deduction for one-half of self-employment tax.** Multiply line 5 by 50% (.50). Enter the result here and on **Form 1040, line 27,** or **Form 1040NR, line 27** **6**		

For Paperwork Reduction Act Notice, see your tax return instructions. Cat. No. 11358Z **Schedule SE (Form 1040) 2010**

Name of person with **self-employment** income (as shown on Form 1040) | Social security number of person with **self-employment** income ▶

Section B—Long Schedule SE

Part I Self-Employment Tax

Note. If your only income subject to self-employment tax is **church employee income,** see page SE-3 for specific instructions. Also see page SE-1 for the definition of church employee income.

A	If you are a minister, member of a religious order, or Christian Science practitioner **and** you filed Form 4361, but you had $400 or more of **other** net earnings from self-employment, check here and continue with Part I ▶ ☐			
1a	Net farm profit or (loss) from Schedule F, line 36, and farm partnerships, Schedule K-1 (Form 1065), box 14, code A. **Note.** Skip lines 1a and 1b if you use the farm optional method (see page SE-5)	1a		
b	If you received social security retirement or disability benefits, enter the amount of Conservation Reserve Program payments included on Schedule F, line 6b, or listed on Schedule K-1 (Form 1065), box 20, code Y	1b	(	)
2	Net profit or (loss) from Schedule C, line 31; Schedule C-EZ, line 3; Schedule K-1 (Form 1065), box 14, code A (other than farming); and Schedule K-1 (Form 1065-B), box 9, code J1. Ministers and members of religious orders, see page SE-1 for types of income to report on this line. See page SE-4 for other income to report. **Note.** Skip this line if you use the nonfarm optional method (see page SE-5)	2		
3	Combine lines 1a, 1b, and 2. Subtract from that total the amount on Form 1040, line 29, or Form 1040NR, line 29, and enter the result (see page SE-3)	3		
4a	If line 3 is more than zero, multiply line 3 by 92.35% (.9235). Otherwise, enter amount from line 3	4a		
	Note. If line 4a is less than $400 due to Conservation Reserve Program payments on line 1b, see page SE-3.			
b	If you elect one or both of the optional methods, enter the total of lines 15 and 17 here	4b		
c	Combine lines 4a and 4b. If less than $400, **stop**; you do not owe self-employment tax. **Exception.** If less than $400 and you had **church employee income,** enter -0- and continue ▶	4c		
5a	Enter your **church employee income** from Form W-2. See page SE-1 for definition of church employee income 5a			
b	Multiply line 5a by 92.35% (.9235). If less than $100, enter -0-	5b		
6	Add lines 4c and 5b	6		
7	Maximum amount of combined wages and self-employment earnings subject to social security tax or the 6.2% portion of the 7.65% railroad retirement (tier 1) tax for 2010	7	106,800	00
8a	Total social security wages and tips (total of boxes 3 and 7 on Form(s) W-2) and railroad retirement (tier 1) compensation. If $106,800 or more, skip lines 8b through 10, and go to line 11 . . . 8a			
b	Unreported tips subject to social security tax (from Form 4137, line 10) 8b			
c	Wages subject to social security tax (from Form 8919, line 10) 8c			
d	Add lines 8a, 8b, and 8c	8d		
9	Subtract line 8d from line 7. If zero or less, enter -0- here and on line 10 and go to line 11 ▶	9		
10	Multiply the **smaller** of line 6 or line 9 by 12.4% (.124)	10		
11	Multiply line 6 by 2.9% (.029)	11		
12	**Self-employment tax.** Add lines 10 and 11. Enter here and on **Form 1040, line 56,** or **Form 1040NR, line 54**	12		
13	**Deduction for one-half of self-employment tax.** Multiply line 12 by 50% (.50). Enter the result here and on **Form 1040, line 27, or Form 1040NR, line 27** . . 13			

Part II Optional Methods To Figure Net Earnings (see page SE-4)

Farm Optional Method. You may use this method **only** if **(a)** your gross farm income[1] was not more than $6,720, **or (b)** your net farm profits[2] were less than $4,851.

14	Maximum income for optional methods	14	4,480	00
15	Enter the **smaller** of: two-thirds (²/₃) of gross farm income[1] (not less than zero) **or** $4,480. Also include this amount on line 4b above	15		

Nonfarm Optional Method. You may use this method **only** if **(a)** your net nonfarm profits[3] were less than $4,851 and also less than 72.189% of your gross nonfarm income,[4] **and (b)** you had net earnings from self-employment of at least $400 in 2 of the prior 3 years. **Caution.** You may use this method no more than five times.

16	Subtract line 15 from line 14	16		
17	Enter the **smaller** of: two-thirds (²/₃) of gross nonfarm income[4] (not less than zero) **or** the amount on line 16. Also include this amount on line 4b above	17		

[1] From Sch. F, line 11, and Sch. K-1 (Form 1065), box 14, code B.

[2] From Sch. F, line 36, and Sch. K-1 (Form 1065), box 14, code A—minus the amount you would have entered on line 1b had you not used the optional method.

[3] From Sch. C, line 31; Sch. C-EZ, line 3; Sch. K-1 (Form 1065), box 14, code A; and Sch. K-1 (Form 1065-B), box 9, code J1.

[4] From Sch. C, line 7; Sch. C-EZ, line 1; Sch. K-1 (Form 1065), box 14, code C; and Sch. K-1 (Form 1065-B), box 9, code J2.

Home Office Tax Deduction

If you use one room of your home exclusively for your business, you will probably qualify for a home office tax deduction. This can reduce the amount of taxes you owe. The word "exclusive" is meant very literally. You cannot use a room for business during the day and as a family room at night. Although you cannot claim your kitchen table, your home office need not be an entire room. You can designate one section of a room for business and even without a physical separation claim the space as a home office.

The size of your home office will determine the deduction you can claim. For example, if you use 10 percent of the living space you can deduct 10 percent of your utilities, real estate taxes, mortgage interest, etc. The cost of furniture, paint, and rugs can also be deducted. However, your business must be making a profit and your deductions cannot exceed the income from your business.

Many accountants have advised their clients not to take the home office deduction for two reasons: First, this deduction is a "red flag" that could trigger an audit. Second, claiming depreciation on part of your house lowers the amount you can claim you paid for your home, which can mean a larger taxable profit when you sell it. You won't be able to defer tax on the part of the profit that is attributable to the office space. So, consult your tax preparer before taking even a valid home office deduction. For more information, get IRS Publication 587, "Business Use of Your Home," at www.irs.gov.

Most Common Mail Order Business Planning Questions

Q: What is the ideal mail order product?

A: An ideal mail order product is easy to mail, unique, desired by a well-defined target market, inexpensive to buy or produce, can be sold for at least four times your cost, and is easy to describe. There is one product that meets all of these conditions and allows you exclusive rights and full control over your production. That product is information. If you have expertise in any field, you can transform that knowledge into newsletters, books, booklets, audiotapes, videotapes, manuals, and more. Printed and recorded materials that cost little to produce can be sold for $5 to $5,000 or more, depending on the exclusivity of the material. Your customers will not be paying for printed paper or the cost of the tape. They will be buying your expertise. You can act as a consultant and provide your services over the telephone, via fax, or on the Internet. Information is also the best product to sell online (see chapter 9).

Q: There are companies that offer products for mail order sales. Can this be profitable?

A: There are many companies that provide access to hundreds of products that can be sold via mail order. They usually give you the opportunity to buy their catalogs and give you a code number for placing orders. Giftware items are usually featured. To be successful in mail order, you must have a sincere interest in what you are selling and a clear picture of your target audience. If you can find a company that offers high-quality, unique merchandise that will appeal to a carefully defined market, and you are allowed enough of a profit margin, you could consider becoming an agent for this type of company. Although some people have made money with this type of opportunity, it is not recommended.

Q: How many products do I need to sell in order to be successful?

A: You can begin your business with one product that has been carefully targeted to appeal to a well-researched market. It is unlikely, however, that you can sustain success if you don't have follow-up products or services to offer. Selling just one product is a waste of your market research.

Q: If I don't want to apply for a loan, why do I need a business plan?

A: You can't build a house without a blueprint or plan a trip without knowing your route. You can't build a business or know which direction to choose unless you have a business plan. You need to have goals and create step-by-step plans for reaching those goals. You have to understand your product and your target market. It is important to plan how you will finance your business and how long it will take to make a profit. You have to know who will help you do all of the jobs involved in running your business.

Q: I am still working full-time as an employee while I am getting my mail order business going. Can I file a tax return for my regular job and as a business owner at the same time?

A: Yes. You will file Schedule C for your business activities along with Form 1040.

Q: What should I do if I have questions about my federal tax return?

A: The Internal Revenue Service office nearest you may have a help line. Look in your local telephone book or call (800) 829-1040 (online, www.irs.gov). The IRS also has publications on a variety of small-business topics, such as Business Use of Your Home (587) and Tax Guide for Small Business (334). Your library may have these publications available, or you can write to the IRS at 1111 Constitution Avenue, NW, Washington, DC 20224.

Q: What is the most important thing I can do to ensure my success in my home-based mail order business?

A: If making money is your only goal, your chances for success will be diminished. We each have a unique talent. Find yours, and use it to enhance the products or services that hold special meaning for you. If the result is something that can help others solve a problem or fulfill a desire, you will have put yourself in the perfect position to become successful. Allow your business concept to take on a life of its own, evolve, and grow as you work on it. Believe in the business you create, and don't let outside influences discourage you. Most businesses fail because their owners give up. Persistence always pays.

04 Creating No-Fail Direct Mail

Close your eyes and imagine how much money you could make in mail order if you could put information about your business in the hands of thousands of your potential customers right now. Now open your eyes and get busy: This is a dream that can come true! The largest and most successful mail order companies still use direct mail as their promotional method of choice, even in our high-tech environment. Promoting by mail has endured because it is the most cost-effective and targeted way to attract new customers and reach out to existing ones. Like the mouse that roared, your home-based business can use the same techniques as the lions of industry to produce direct-mail promotions that generate a high percentage of sales.

Before you begin to promote your product or service through the mail, you must understand that direct mail is different from any other type of promotion. Big-business mailers painstakingly plan and test every element that goes into the offers they send to their lists of carefully chosen names. They are constantly refining their direct-mail techniques, and word of success spreads quickly throughout the industry. Can a home business owner like you hope to access any of these secrets? You sure can.

Not only can you find out the most current direct-mail research, but you can also design your own free home-study course. Your first step is to get your name on as many mailing lists as possible. Write away for free information every time you see an offer that is related to your field of interest. Save all the mail you receive for at least one month, and then spread it all out on a large table. Pay special attention to the mail sent by the most successful and prolific companies, for they will be sure to include the best and most proven elements in their packages.

As you analyze each mailing, look at the typeface, the ink color, and the paper colors. What type of paper is used? How is the copy written? There is a reason for every piece of paper in the mailing, including the envelope. Watch for the words, colors, and types of inserts that appear in many of the mailings. As your collection increases, you will begin to see that each company mails its own version of the same package. The proven methods used by the big guys to generate millions of dollars each year will work for you too.

Your Direct-Mail Package

The average family receives at least ten direct-mail promotions each week. Some active mail order buyers receive more than that each day. One person's junk mail can be another person's treasure. How will your direct-mail promotion be perceived? Your envelope and its contents have seconds to make a quick and effective first impression, or all of your efforts will be dumped. The look, feel, and sound of each insert must attract attention from the moment your precious parcel is lifted from the mailbox. As you open your mail each day, look over your own shoulder and gauge your reactions. What attracts you, and what causes you to put your mail in the circular file?

The good news is that you don't have to play guessing games when you design your promotional package. Because direct mail is the most easily tested form of marketing, experts have been able to determine what types of inserts produce maximum response. You can do your own testing to make sure that your package is the best it can be. Test the look of your mailing and the copy to see what works and what doesn't. Change a headline, an ink color, or a price, and track the response. You might be surprised at the increase or decrease in response. Test only one element at a time, so you will know what is causing the change.

Although there is room for some creativity, the classic direct-mail package contains the following essential elements:

Outer envelope. Almost every direct-mail expert will advise you to put "teaser" copy on the outside of your envelope to entice the prospect to open it up. I disagree for two reasons. Envelope copy such as "Look inside to learn how to save money in the supermarket" can be effective sometimes. But if you put such copy on the outside of the envelope, you save the recipient the trouble of opening the letter before deciding whether to throw it away. And if the teaser copy does not live up to expectations, the readers will be disappointed, and you will lose their trust. I don't write on the outside of my personal business correspondence; do you?

Instead, I suggest using a good-quality envelope with an address that has been printed directly on the envelope without a label. If labels are necessary, they should match the color of the envelope. Real stamps, instead of a machine stamp, also add to the personal touch. Don't put a post office box without a company name as your return address. It makes it look like you are trying to hide something. Either put your complete return address on the envelope, or leave it off entirely.

A letter. Direct mail touches your prospect where he or she lives. To obtain full benefit from this personal touch, a letter will always be at the heart of a classic direct-mail package. You may be tempted to put your letter on fancy stationery and use a sophisticated typeface. This would be a mistake. If you study the direct-mail promotions you've received, you will note that most are put on plain white paper with a typeface that resembles that of a typewriter. Your letter must be simple to read, but this is no casual communication.

There are four main ingredients inherent in every successful direct-mail letter: It must (1) attract attention, (2) clearly explain the benefits to your potential customer, (3) overcome any possible objections, and (4) call the reader to action. To help you remember these objectives as you write your letter, let me introduce two friends who are well known in the direct-mail industry: AIDA (**A**ttention, **I**nterest, **D**esire, and **A**ction), and the one all of your potential customers know really well, WIIFM (**W**hat's **I**n **I**t **F**or **M**e?).

How long should a letter be? Long enough to get the job done. If you have a long message, don't hesitate to write a long letter. If people are interested in what you have to sell, they will read every word. Tradition says that long letters work better than short letters, especially on high-ticket items.

A brochure. Your brochure is an extension of your letter. It gives you a place to tell the story of your product with pictures and additional details. Some people are visually oriented. They will look at the pictures first and then decide if they should read the rest of your package. Others want to read the offer first and then, after reading all the benefits, they will look at the brochure to see what the product looks like.

Your product's key benefits should be emphasized in your brochure. The photos you use should never be unpleasant or hard to look at, even if you are using fear as a motivator to buy. An alarm company would gain more by using a picture of a happy and safe family than an intruder lurking in the darkness outside the window.

You might want to include questions and answers and testimonials from satisfied customers. Print a guarantee in a framed box that looks official. If you

Dear Reader,

Will your direct-mail promotions convince your customers to buy? Yes—here's how. Involve your reader by asking a question. Your letter is your most important sales piece, and the first paragraph will make or break interest. Use the first paragraph to promise a benefit.

Next, enlarge on this benefit and tell readers what they will get. Back up your claims with proof and testimonials. Then tell them what they will lose if they don't order. People don't like to be left out.

Each paragraph should be indented and short—no more than seven lines. All letters should be printed in a typewriter typeface to give them a personalized look. Sure, your reader knows that you didn't type it yourself, but it works anyway. Short, "handwritten" notes in the left margin will be read.

To increase your chances of hitting the jackpot, use white paper with black type for your sales letter—except your signature, which can be blue. The typeface should never be smaller than ten points.

You may want to make important points more
obvious by indenting like this.

THIS IS IMPORTANT . . .

Headings can accent important paragraphs. Don't justify the right margin. Leave it ragged, like a real letter. You don't want it to look like a computerized message. And since you want your prospect to turn the page, never let the first page end with a completed sentence.

Your most important benefits can be highlighted by putting them in a list preceded by bullets. Here are some important things to remember about writing a direct-mail letter that works:

- Make your salutation as specific as possible. "Dear Parent" is much better than "Dear Friend."
- Use simple language, and be friendly. Formal copy may intimidate your reader.
- Picture one member of your target audience and write directly to that person.
- Appeal to your prospect's emotions, not logic.
- Empathize with your reader. You know what he or she wants or needs, because you share those traits.

To end your letter, rephrase the benefits and then tell your prospects exactly what you want them to do. A call to action is the proper way to end this very effective marketing piece. So don't delay. It is important to get started writing your letter right now.

Sincerely yours,

Georganne Fiumara

Georganne Fiumara

P.S. Don't forget: After the salutation and the first paragraph, the P.S. is the third part of the letter that is read. Use it for emphasizing an important benefit or restating an offer.

are offering many benefits, number them and include a list. Even though you are using words, your brochure should present the words in an appealing graphic presentation.

The more expensive your product, the more elaborate your brochure must be. High-quality paper and possibly four-color printing may be indicated.

A response form. Your package should have a separate response form that fits into your reply envelope. It should be easy to use and easy to fill out. Your telephone number should be listed in case the prospect wants to ask a question or order by telephone.

A reply envelope. Many businesses enclose postage-paid envelopes for ordering. Even if you don't supply postage, the addressed reply envelope is an essential component of your direct-mail package. You want your readers to act as soon as they read your package. If they have to look for an envelope first, they may put it down and have second thoughts. That is the simple reason why a reply envelope must be included in your direct-mail package.

If you want to enclose a postage-paid, business-reply card or envelope in your package, you have to get a permit and a permit number from the post office. There is an annual fee for the permit. Then your permit number will be printed on the face of your reply-mail envelope in accordance with postal regulations. When your reply mail is delivered, you will have to pay the postage plus a surcharge. Consult your post office for current rates. Be warned: Responders can enclose anything they want in your envelopes, and you will still have to pay the postage.

Optional enclosures include the following:

A discount coupon. Offering your prospects a special deal and a deadline to meet will encourage them to respond without delay.

A lift letter. A lift letter is sometimes an overused device. It is a folded piece of paper (about 6 inches by 8 inches) that says something like: "If you have decided not to order, read this." Inside is a short letter, usually signed by someone other than the person who signed the sales letter. The message addresses the reader's skepticism and sales resistance: "I understand why you might feel that this offer is too good to be true. I felt the same way when I heard about it." Lift letters may not be effective in business-to-business promotions.

Words that Work

There are certain words and phrases that help elicit response when they are included in your direct-mail copy. Use these power words, and you will make more sales. Here is a partial list:

free	you	today	miracle	take a minute
save	now	hurry	guaranteed	don't gamble
new	win	how to	opportunity	now you can . . .
private	easy	success	announcing	treat yourself
special	quick	safe	a new you	step-by-step
fun	bonus	discover	never before	introducing
love	money	proven	tested	last chance

It Is in the Cards

Postcards

Want to send a promotion to your house list without spending a lot of money? Consider postcards. Used creatively, postcards can attract attention and produce results. You can use many of the direct-mail principles in postcards, and they require less production and postage, even though they are an effective sales tool.

Postcards can be oversized and have elaborate four-color pictures, or they can be fast and easy. You can write and design a postcard on your computer, get it photocopied or quick-printed, and have it in the mail in two days. The higher quality cards can do some prospecting for you. Mail them to a list of prospects and put a toll-free telephone number on it for response. Use a "quickie" postcard to drum up some fast cash. Mail them to your customers, and make an offer they can't resist. Or follow up a complete direct-mail package with a postcard reminding your prospects that a deadline is approaching. Because postcards can be printed four to a page and then cut, printing is very affordable.

You can use a postcard as a coupon. Tell your prospects to make any corrections to their name and address and enclose the postcard with their check to qualify for a special offer. Consider sending a series of postcards containing related messages or teaser copy that is solved by the last postcard. You'll have your readers anticipating your next mailing.

Postcards are little billboards of information that people tend to save. Have blank postcards printed with your business name so that you can drop a message to a colleague, answer a quick question, or send a thank-you message.

PROFIT PROFILE: Phyllis L. Cox, Artist

The best way to make money by mail is by selling a service or publishing information. Phyllis Cox does both. She has taken what is usually a local service and has offered it on a national basis. Phyllis is a desktop publisher, graphic designer, and artist. She helps individuals and organizations handle all of their printed materials, from concept to design through printing, and offers unique specialty cards and invitations.

Her national career began in 1987, when she was profiled in an article that appeared in a large-circulation women's magazine. She received many letters and telephone calls asking for her help but found it difficult to communicate design concepts across the miles—at first. The addition of a fax machine helped solve that problem back then and she still uses it today. But now, she is also able to email proofs to her customers.

Her promotional postcard (see opposite) follows the most important rule for direct-mail marketing: It relates benefits. The card, printed in black and red ink on white card stock, makes a promise on the front that many small-business owners would love to hear: YOU'LL NEVER HAVE TO GO TO THE PRINTER AGAIN! The flip side of her oversize card (8½ inches by 5½ inches) demonstrates Phyllis's graphic abilities by its own appealing design and logo. She tells her prospects that they will save time, money, and stress by using her services—benefits that her target audience finds hard to resist.

Phyllis has a working agreement with a local printer that allows her to offer very competitive prices. She offers free pickup and delivery on a local basis, and printing shipments can be delivered via UPS across the country.

To contact Phyllis, e-mail her at PLCartist@aol.com.

Sample Promotional Postcard

PHYLLIS L. COX
ARTIST

2703 FALCON STREET
EAST MEADOW, NY 11554

YOU'LL NEVER HAVE TO GO TO THE PRINTER AGAIN!

FORMS • NEWSLETTERS • FLIERS • BUSINESS CARDS • STATIONERY • JOURNALS • BROCHURES

MANUALS • RESUMES • RUBBER STAMPS • INVITATIONS

PHYLLIS L. COX
ARTIST

FAX or PHONE
516/826-1294

e-mail: PLCdesigns@aol.com

HAVE YOU BEEN SEARCHING FOR AN EASY WAY TO HANDLE YOUR TYPESETTING, DESIGN AND PRINTING NEEDS?

YOUR SEARCH IS OVER!!!

Save time, money and stress – I'll do it all...and I'll come to you!
Call today for low prices, on-time delivery and very personalized service.

From Concept to Design to Print

ENVELOPES ADDRESSED • MAILING LISTS • CERTIFICATES

• Logos • Graphic Design • Typesetting • Printing

Self-Mailers

A self-mailer is a double postcard that is folded over. One side contains the sales message and the other is a postage-paid response card that the prospect detaches and mails back to you. You can use many of the devices you've learned about writing a direct-mail letter and brochure, but on a smaller scale. Or you can make the sales portion look more like a display ad in a magazine. In either case an interesting headline on the address portion will get the prospect to open the card and read your message.

A self-mailer can be more effective than a postcard but less effective than your classic direct-mail package. If the cost is prohibiting you from sending a complete package, a self-mailer can save you money. However, unless you accept credit cards or send bills as magazines do when they sell subscriptions, you can only use a self-mailer to solicit a response, not a sale. If the prospect has to put the response portion in his or her own envelope and enclose a check, you probably will not elicit the response you desire.

Card Packs

You can place your offer in a card pack that is mailed to specific target audiences. It is like placing an ad, but an actual package of individual cards is sent to the prospect. Your offer will be sandwiched in with other offers. Participating in a card pack can be cost-effective, but you should ask to see a sample first and do research on the people who will be receiving the package.

The best use of a card pack is for two-step advertising. Because space is limited, you want the prospect to call you or return the card for additional information. An offer of free information will work best here. Make your offer short and sweet. Don't use tiny type to get more information on the card. Instead make an offer, relate a benefit, picture your product or free offering, and ask for a response. One side should be a business-reply card addressed to you. To save space, have the prospect fill in name, address, and telephone number in the upper left-hand side where the return address is usually placed.

Creating a Catalog

It is not necessary to have a catalog when you first begin your mail order business. Catalogs are expensive to produce, and if the information on one page changes, it could make the entire catalog obsolete. You are just getting to know your target audience, and you need to have some room for flexibility. At start-up, it is likely that you will have only one or two products. Product promotion sheets, flyers, or a brochure contained in a classic direct-mail package may be a better choice.

Expanding Your Line

Once you have had success with your lead product and have a house list of interested customers, it is time to expand your line with related products. It could also be time to create your first catalog. A catalog needs to be more than pages full of products. If you plan it correctly, it can be a publication your customers and prospects look forward to receiving.

If you are a gardener, you know how important seed catalogs are to you in the cold winter months. While leafing through the pages, you are transported to a warmer, more appealing place. Catalogs can be the stuff dreams are made of. They can also be entertaining and informative. Some catalogs feature a fictional family or an appealing couple whose house is full of items from the catalog. The pictures show how the items are being used. Other catalogs actually tell a story that is continued in each new edition. Pages of background information about your product area can encourage your reader to use and save your catalog.

Your catalog should have a personality. It is not unusual for smaller companies to put a picture of the business owner along with a letter to the readers. This promotes a feeling of friendliness. You can even print letters from customers on this page, creating a give-and-take. The descriptions below the product photographs or illustrations could be written as recommendations from the people pictured or from you personally.

Unlike an advertisement, catalog copy needs to make the complete sale, so all information about your products and how to order should be made clear. To promote sales, coupons with deadlines can be used. Indicating that quantities are limited (when they actually are) can also provoke a quicker sale.

Start Small

Your catalog does not have to be on glossy paper with full-color photographs in the beginning. If your items appeal to a targeted group of people, a simple catalog can produce results. You don't need flash, but you do need substance. A toll-free number, credit card acceptance, and outstanding customer service are essential to any catalog. People shop by mail because it is convenient. Make convenience your number-one benefit, and you will attract more sales.

Here are a few more tips to consider when you create your catalog:

- The big catalogs market big. When starting out, choose a market niche and aim your catalog at its members' needs.
- Planning is key. Before creating your catalog, make an outline of everything that will be in it. Don't forget your guarantee and all ordering instructions. Decide on the format. Choose the size, typeface, and paper size.
- All of the elements in your catalog must create an image. Make sure that your theme is carried out on every page.
- Put your ordering telephone number on every catalog page.

Getting into Another Company's Catalog

If yours is an original product that only you offer, it can be easier and less expensive for you to get your product into another company's catalog. Before that can happen, you have to know what catalogs are available and which ones are aimed at your target audience. To accomplish this, get a copy of the *Catalog of Catalogs* (Woodbine House), and make a mailing list of appropriate catalogs.

If you don't have a brochure that clearly shows your product, have a color catalog sheet printed. Print your track record on the back. Include the number of units that have been sold and the way the sales were made. Of course, you want the catalogs you are targeting to know all of the benefits and features your product has to offer.

Before you mail your package, call the catalog company and get the name of the current buyer. Ask to receive instructions for submitting products for consideration.

Don't send a sample of your product at first. Wait until the buyer shows an interest. The buyer will want all the details such as size, composition, packaging, and wholesale cost, as well as your assurance that you have the ability to fill a large number of orders. Catalog companies usually expect delivery of products two to three weeks after sending you a purchase order. It can take up to six months for the acceptance process, so be prepared to go the long haul.

Some catalog companies will buy your product outright. Others will take it on consignment. Some companies charge a fee for placing your product in their catalogs. Only you can decide if the potential profit will justify the expense.

PROFIT PROFILE: Ann Morris Enterprises

Starting a home-based mail order business can be difficult, and each of us has days when we feel that we are not up to the task. The next time you feel that way, think of Ann Morris. Ann always wanted to run her own business, and she has succeeded despite the fact that she is totally blind. Her catalog of 500 items for the visually impaired has annual gross sales of more than $260,000.

Ann's mail order business began in 1986, when she invented two products that help the visually impaired: a handmade writing aid called an OptaGuide and an audible battery tester that works with the sound of a buzzer instead of a meter. Today her catalog is filled with more of her inventions, such as special wallets to help keep track of money and talking thermometers. She is always on the lookout for new products to include in the catalog.

Ann began her business as many others do. While attending classes at a local community college, she began to promote her original inventions and placed ads in magazines and newsletters for the visually impaired. Initial sales were good, so she started distributing her products through catalogs and sent direct-mail promotions to 500 schools and agencies that serve the visually impaired. Initial sales as high as $2,000 in one month were encouraging.

Her first catalog, done in large-print format with line drawings of products, went out to a list of 1,700 names. Today, she mails up to 45,000 of her catalogs per year. Her in-house list pulls a 10 percent response. So far she has not been successful with rented lists. New names for her house list come from ads in periodicals for the visually impaired.

Ann had to buy a new house to accommodate her business. One full floor and the basement are devoted to it, including offices and warehouse space. She became successful because she fully understood and knew where to reach her target market and provided needed and appealing products.

For more information, go to www.AnnMorris.com.

Printing Basics

Printing is an integral part of direct mail. Your printed materials are the only representatives of your business when they are sent through the mail to your prospects. Your choices of paper, ink color, and design will influence the look of your printed pieces and how much your printing will cost. If you understand the basics of print production, you will be better equipped to handle this ongoing aspect of your direct-mail program.

You may not be able to repair your own car, but if you know something about car repair, you can speak to the mechanic with intelligence. Getting your materials printed is a lot like that. You have to have a basic knowledge of printing before you try to find a printer who can guide you through the process. You may have to try a few different printers before you find one you can trust. And you need to have some basic knowledge about printing before you make your choices.

The number of ink colors and the quality of the paper you choose will be the most important factors contributing to your cost. If you want four-color photographs, you will probably get the best price and the best results by using one of the national companies that specialize in that type of printing. A list of such companies is contained in the appendix.

If you have the skill and the equipment, the pieces you want printed can be designed right on your computer. If you do not do desktop publishing or typesetting, you will have to hire a graphic designer or use the services provided by your printer.

When ordering printing, remember the following:

- Printers double the prices of the paper they buy and the outside services they use, such as typesetting. If you can purchase paper at wholesale prices or commission your own typesetting and design, you can save money.
- Get an estimate before you hire a printer or a graphic artist. Be sure of your facts and figures, or the estimate will be high.
- Get two or three estimates and tell each printer that you are shopping around.
- Provide your copy to your graphic artist on disk so that it does not have to be retyped.
- Most printers require ten days to complete a job.

In Search of a Name and Address

Before you drop your perfect package in the mail, make sure that the name on the envelope represents the bull's-eye of your target market. Experts say that the quality of the list selection counts for 60 to 80 percent of a mailing's success. Postage and printed materials can be expensive, and you don't want to have your mailing sent to anyone who has not demonstrated an interest in your type of products.

Large corporate mailers can invest in carefully tested mailing-list rentals, but that might not be the smartest first step for your business. Rented lists are expensive and are not always what they promise. It is possible to compile your own list by obtaining alumni directories; wedding, birth, and engagement notices in the newspaper; subscriber lists to special-interest publications—whatever will help put you in touch with your target audience. Never forget that the names of the people who have already placed an order or have written to you to request information—your house list—are your best prospects. A good response rate from a rented mailing list is rarely higher than 1 to 4 percent. Your house list can pull 5 to 15 percent or higher. These figures are important if you consider the size of your mailing. For every 1,000 pieces mailed to your house mailing list, you could expect 50 to 150 orders. An untried list might attract only 10 to 40 orders. As you can see, you would have to mail thousands of promotions in order to elicit enough orders to make a profit from rented lists.

Creating a "House" List

As we've discussed, your house list is made up of the people who have contacted you in some way to ask for your information. Your house list will always give you the highest rate of response to any promotion. Offering free information or a sample product through advertising or publicity is the best way to build a house list.

Renting Mailing Lists

List brokers rent lists of names and addresses in every imaginable category: age, occupation, hobbies, buying habits, and so on. Costs for these lists average $50–$100 per 1,000 names for one-time use, and most list managers require a 5,000-name minimum order. This is the smallest number of names that experts say can be tested with accurate results.

Rental lists fall into two main categories: compiled and direct response. Compiled lists, taken from telephone books and other directories, can work, but you might not have to rent one. There are national lists from telephone books available on CD that can be sorted into many categories, such as flower shops, accountants, people with the same last name, and so on. When you purchase such a program, you can use it at will. Updates are available on a quarterly basis.

Direct-response lists consist of subscribers to special-interest magazines, people who have purchased well-defined products, or members of national organizations. Many lists are enhanced, making telephone numbers, gender, number of children, income range, and age information available to the potential renter. These are called selects, and you will usually pay a little more when you take advantage of them. You can rent a list of the subscribers of a magazine or request women subscribers with children under age three. Using selects helps you to target your market more accurately.

Never rent more than 5,000 names before you test the list to see what type of response it will elicit. And be careful. Renting a list can be a little bit like buying a used car. It may look good, but you never really know how it will run until you have it checked out. You can make some expensive mistakes if you are not careful. Resources in the appendix will help you find the most targeted lists available.

How to Choose a Mailing List

The following list of questions will help you evaluate a mailing list you are considering renting. The correct answer to every question is "yes."

1. Are the names on this list part of your target audience?
2. Do these people have proven buying potential?
3. Were the names acquired by direct mail?
4. Are the names recently acquired?
5. Can selections for age, income, gender, and so forth be made?
6. Do other companies order more names after testing the list?
7. Is the list clean? (Does it contain few bad addresses or duplicates?)
8. Is the list available in a format you can use?

When to Mail, When Not to Mail

When you mail is almost as important as *what* you mail. Results will vary slightly according to your type of offer, but the direct-mail industry has determined that you will get the highest response rate when mailing in January. February is a close second, followed in order by October, August, November, September, December, July, March, April, May, and June. You will have to test to see if your customers follow this pattern.

Conventional wisdom says never mail your promotions so that they are received on the first day of the month, because people have bills to pay. This could be true, but I say if they have their checkbooks out, they just might write a check to you at the same time.

Predicting Response

On Election Day, we watch the television networks predict who our new president will be almost immediately after the polls close. These predictions are based on statistical analysis of the responses given by a relatively few people who are questioned as they exit the polls. That small statistical sampling almost always is predictive of the actual vote.

Just as it is possible to correctly predict the outcome of an election after only a small percentage of the results has been tabulated, there are proven methods and statistical formulas that will help you predict the number of responses you will receive to a promotion.

There are all sorts of equations you can use to predict response to a mailing, an advertisement, or publicity you have received. When Mothers' Home Business Network receives publicity in a national publication, I multiply the number of responses the first week by twenty. I'm not sure where I originally heard that formula, but it works. I usually have a pretty good estimate of how much mail will be received within one year. About half of the responses arrive within the first four weeks, and the largest day of response is always the second Monday.

When you send out a direct-mail promotion or a catalog, you can expect to receive 50 percent of your orders ten days after receiving your first response.

We all think that we are individuals who act according to our own timetables. As you can see, this is not true. Almost everything we do is predictable. If you want to be able to track the success of your promotions and predict response, you have to keep detailed records.

Recording Response

When you first start your business, you probably don't care where your orders come from as long as you make some sales. But it is important to know what works and what doesn't. You want to be prepared to answer all your mail and telephone calls, so it is helpful to predict the ultimate number of responses. Careful records are the only way you can keep track on a daily basis.

When you are just starting out, you can keep track of outgoing and incoming mail on your planning calendar. But once you have many active promotions, you need a separate monthly record for each one. If you put a key code in each of your ads and the various direct-mail promotions you try, you will be able to see clearly what is producing for you.

Direct-Mail Checklist

- ❐ Gather as many direct-mail packages as possible, especially from successful companies. Analyze their methods and adapt them.
- ❐ When writing your letter, picture one member of your target audience and speak directly to that person.
- ❐ Keep your paragraphs short. None should have more than seven lines.
- ❐ Use simple language and be friendly. Formal copy may intimidate your reader.
- ❐ Make your salutation as specific as possible. "Dear Parent" is much better than "Dear Friend."
- ❐ Your headline and your first paragraph should grab the reader's attention.
- ❐ Use a P.S. and make sure it conveys a unique benefit or refers to a discount or deadline.
- ❐ Empathize with your reader. You know what he or she wants or needs because you share those traits.
- ❐ Make sure your letters use AIDA (**A**ttention, **I**nterest, **D**esire, and **A**ction) and WIIFM (**W**hat's **I**n **I**t **F**or **M**e?).
- ❐ Produce your direct-mail letter using a typewriter-style typeface in black ink on white paper.
- ❐ Create a brochure that illustrates and elaborates on your letter.
- ❐ Design a response form that is easy to understand and complete.
- ❐ Include a reply envelope, even if it does not have postage.
- ❐ Offer a discount or other special deal with a deadline to increase response.
- ❐ Use power words in all your promotions.
- ❐ To save time and money, try postcard promotions, self-mailers, or card packs.
- ❐ Don't produce a catalog until you have an established lead product.
- ❐ Your first catalog should not be glossy and expensive.
- ❐ Use your catalog to establish a relationship with your audience.
- ❐ Try getting a product you produce in another company's catalog.

- ❒ Take time to learn about printing.
- ❒ Always promote to your house list first. It will elicit the highest response.
- ❒ If you rent a mailing list, test at least 5,000 names before ordering more.
- ❒ Mail during the prime months for direct response.
- ❒ Always key code your mailings.
- ❒ Keep records of mailings and the response you receive so that you can repeat a successful mailing.

On the top of your monthly record, keep all the necessary information for repeating the promotion. Write down all pertinent data, including what was enclosed in each promotional package. Your record should begin on the first day you receive responses.

Importance of Follow-up

Did you receive a good response to your mailing? Great—but don't stop there. It is time to follow up. Send the same promotion to the same list, and you can expect a response equal to about 60 percent of your first response. Change the cover of your catalog and response rates could increase or decrease. Mailing just once to a good prospect is one of the biggest mistakes small businesses make.

Don't forget to put your money where your market is: Those who placed an order should be sent regular mailings offering additional, related products. Did you know that it costs up to five times more to sell to new prospects than it costs to sell to your active customers?

Common Mailing List Questions

Q: If I rent a mailing list, should I mail to all the names at once?

A: Most mailing-list rental agreements require that you rent at least 5,000 names and mail to them all at the same time. If you want to space your mailings, rent only the number of names you can use immediately.

Q: Mailing lists are usually rented for one-time use only. How will the renter know if I use the names again?

A: When mailing lists are rented, they are "seeded" with names of people who are there for the purpose of reporting what direct-mail materials they receive and how often. These names are put there to prevent unauthorized use; however, when someone on the list places an order or contacts you in some other way, that name becomes yours to use as many times as you wish.

Q: You say a letter is so important. What will happen if I just send a brochure without a letter?

A: The direct-mail letter personalizes your mailing. Even though the recipients know that you didn't write it directly to them, it still works. A mailing without a letter leaves a void that is impossible to fill.

05 Mail Order Marketing Basics

What is the single most important aspect of your mail order business? Your products? No. Good products are an essential ingredient, but you will not sell one item if your potential customers do not know about your business. To make those sales you have to let the customers know what you have to offer. Marketing is everything you do to attract the attention of your target audience. Paid advertising, direct mail promotions, and public relations are the main tools you will use to get your message out and create a company image. But as a smart marketer, you won't stop there.

To be a successful mail order marketer, you will keep your feet firmly planted in the traditional methods and then look to the stars for online marketing opportunities. This blending of proven marketing techniques with the new and exciting opportunities available online is the best way to go. Those who shun the tried and true for today's fad ultimately regret their choice. Conversely, staying old-school and ignoring the opportunities available online is also a big mistake. Thinking of new ways to attract customers can become a twenty-four-hour-a-day, seven-days-a-week obsession, but what fun it is when one of your efforts scores! Yes, marketing can be as much fun as winning the lottery but before you begin, you must have a plan.

The Essential First Step: Creating a Marketing Plan

Writing a marketing plan is like writing a business plan, but a lot more interesting. Beginning can be as simple as writing one or two concise paragraphs that describe your business and define who your customers are, what their needs are, why they would want to purchase your products, and when and how you plan to reach them. Then, after determining the amount of money you will have to spend on marketing you will choose the marketing methods that will be the most effective. Don't let a lack of cash stop you from creating a marketing plan. As you will see, some of the most effective marketing does not require much cash, and you should have your plans in place so that you will be ready when more money does become available.

To begin, first, write a short paragraph of no more than fifty words describing your business. The fewer words, the better. Being able to give a concise description of your business is essential to help you relay that information to others. Next, take your most important marketing step: Define your target audience.

Before you can determine exactly who your target market is, you need to know exactly what this term means. Your *target market* is the group of people who is most likely to buy your products. You have to get to know this group intimately if you want to make maximum sales. But why, you might ask, can't you just try to sell your products to as many people as possible? Experts say that if *everyone* is your market, *no one* is your market. It may not seem right, but it is true that the more you define and limit your market, the more products you will sell.

When I started Mothers' Home Business Network, people asked me, "Why just mothers? Why not provide home business information for everyone?" Although I had never heard of target marketing then, I realized that mothers wanted to work at home *so they could spend more time with their children*. This is a motivation that the rest of the population does not have. I was intimately familiar with my target audience because I was a member of that group. All I had to do was analyze my own behavior and motivations, and I instinctively knew how to reach these women and the best way to position the organization.

Through the years, I have seen many general home business publications and organizations start up and eventually fade away. By zeroing in on one small segment of the available market, Mothers' Home Business Network has been able to endure. This narrowed focus is called *niche marketing*.

If you are selling products that you would be interested in purchasing, then you might be a member of your target market. This will help you describe your potential customer before you actually start making sales. At start-up, you can only make educated guesses about the members of your target market. But if you are a member of the group, then you will have more information to use. Once you begin to make sales, you can analyze the people who are actually buying your products by sending out questionnaires and doing other research. Make sure that these people fit into your original concept of your target market, and if they don't, alter your picture.

When you write down your description of members of your target audience, be sure to include the following information: age, gender, type of occupation, income level, marital status, habits, recreational choices, attitudes, needs, desires, and geographic location. What publications do they read? What television and radio programs do they choose? What websites do they visit? If a potential customer fits your profile, don't use distance as a reason for elimination. Mail order allows you to reach out to the entire country and the world.

Once you know who your target audience is, you must position your product in your customers' minds. Slant your marketing so that the customer perceives your products to be just what he or she needs. You do this by creating marketing materials from the point of view of your customers. Don't tell them how good your products are; instead, tell them how much better their lives will be once they purchase your products. The women's perfume ad that shows a handsome man who will be attracted by the scent will be more effective than one showing only a woman holding a bottle. A clothing catalog showing people engaged in interesting activities while wearing the clothes will sell more than a boring catalog with pictures of sweaters. Positioning puts forth the ways your target audience perceives that they will benefit from your products. Your company's name, your logo, or a slogan will help you position your company in customers' minds, even before they actually see your products.

You know who the members of your target audience are and how you want them to perceive your products. Now it is time to find the best ways to reach out to your very carefully targeted potential customers. Should you advertise in the publications they read? Can you obtain a mailing list of these people? Where will you find them on the Internet? Deciding what marketing methods to use and actually creating a tentative schedule of promotions for the year ahead will help you complete your marketing plan. In this chapter, we will focus on how advertising and publicity will help you reach your target audience, and I will give you fifty strategies to keep in mind while you are planning your marketing.

Advertising Your Mail Order Business

If you have a limited marketing budget, I have one thing to tell you about advertising: Don't do it. To be effective, paid advertising in publications and on radio and television needs to be repeated. One-shot ads almost never work, even if they appear in high-response publications. If you can't make a commitment to an advertising campaign, try other marketing methods, such as direct mail or public relations, to promote your business. How much money do you need to launch an advertising campaign? You need enough to buy a minimum of six to nine consecutive ads in the same place. Trying just one or two is a waste of time and money.

When deciding where to spend your marketing dollars, you need to consider your cost per 1,000 prospects (CPM); however, the least expensive CPM is not necessarily your best choice. Direct mail has a high CPM but a much better chance of reaching the members of your target audience, and your sales materials allow you to tell your prospects your complete sales story or send a catalog of your products. It may be smarter to figure your cost per potential buyer. Every business has different needs, and only you can determine if paid advertising should be part of your marketing plan.

If you decide to try advertising, don't choose the most expensive national publications. Test your ideas first locally or in smaller, carefully chosen geographical areas. Some national magazines also offer advertising in regional editions. If you cannot drum up some interest in your products on a local level, you can count on the fact that they will be ignored on a national basis, too. But whatever media outlet you choose, be selective. How many members of your target audience read, watch, or listen to your choice?

The most targeted advertisement I've ever heard of was a promotion for golfers that appeared inside a golf hole. A small daily audience, to be sure, but everyone who saw the ad had an interest in the product. You may not be able to zero in on your market to that extent, but the more targeted your promotion is the higher your rate of response will be. General interest, high-circulation publications do not guarantee high response. Special-interest publications and television and radio shows that interest the members of your target audience can be much better choices. To locate them and find out advertising rates, consult *Standard Rate and Data* service publications, which should be available in your library. It lists all publications by title, includes contact information, and explains the editorial content of each magazine. There are also editions for radio, television, and newspapers.

When you find a publication that is of interest, call or write for its media kit. Complete information about the publication, including the demographics, will be included. The publication will also supply you with an editorial calendar so that you will know which issues may contain articles that feature topics related to your business.

Keep in mind that closing dates for advertisements are two to three months before the issue is published.

Print Classified Ads—Doing the Two-Step

Classified advertising can be powerful when used in the correct way. It is almost impossible to make a sale of more than a few dollars in a classified ad, but you can use this medium to build your mailing list of interested prospects. Offer free information for a self-addressed, stamped envelope. Your prospect will write and request your sales materials. You will send out your package, and you will have a name to add to your house list. This is called *two-step advertising*.

Classified advertising is affordable and should probably be your first attempt at advertising. You will be offered a discount if you purchase space for more than one insertion at a time. Classified advertising, like all other print advertising, needs a good headline. Make sure that yours jumps out and grabs the reader's attention. Words such as "how to" and "free" are always effective. Offering free information about a subject related to your business will attract your potential customers. Make sure that your copy conveys the benefits of your product.

Examine at least twelve back issues of any publication that you are considering. Identify which ads are repeated in each issue. Those ads are the ones that are drawing response. Classified advertising may seem easy, but it is important to remember:

- Don't make your ad too short in order to save money. Instead, try ads of different lengths and with different headlines. Be sure to code the address so that you will know which ads are drawing the most response.
- Choose your ad classification carefully. In fact, you can test the same ads under different headings.
- Emphasize the benefits of your products, not the features.
- If you have a website or e-mail address, be sure to include it in your ad.

Print Display Ads

Display advertising is larger than classified advertising. Sizes range from a full page to a 1-column-inch rectangle. Display ads give you room to use illustrations or a picture of your product, making it possible to bypass the step of sending sales literature. If you are soliciting sales directly from the ad, it is important to provide a method of response, such as an order form or a toll-free telephone number that buyers can call. Since it is easier to make a toll-free call, those who fill out a response coupon might be higher quality prospects.

If you have been successful with a classified ad in a publication, it might be a good place to try a display ad. Research shows that people (both sexes) are most drawn to pictures of babies, pets, and attractive women, in that order. If you can incorporate one or more of these in your ad, it will help you attract attention. (Locomotives are next, but they might be difficult to relate to your campaign.) When writing your ad, write long at first. You must cover all of your product benefits. Then edit your copy so that there is enough white space and room for your illustration.

And remember the following:

- Make sure your headline is effective and eye-catching.
- If possible, don't just show your product, show the product benefit.
- Consider a free offer.
- If the ad is large enough, include a reply coupon, even though you have a toll-free number.
- Reference your website and give the reader a good reason to visit it.

Advertising Online

Be very careful. Advertising online requires knowledge of how your target audience reacts while surfing the Internet. It can get very expensive very quickly if you don't carefully monitor your ads. Although there are many variations, there are three basic ways advertising is purchased online:

1. *CPV (Cost Per Visitor).* Advertisers pay for the number of visitors to the advertiser's website that are generated by the ad.
2. *CPT (Cost Per Thousand).* This method counts each time the Web page with the ad is visited. The advertiser pays a set amount for each 1,000 times the page with the ad is loaded. The advertiser will be charged whether or not the ad is clicked on.
3. *CPC (Cost Per Click).* This is the model used by Google for the ads you see in the right column of their search pages and on individual websites. Advertisers do not initially pay for the ad placement but are charged an agreed upon amount each time someone clicks on the ad to be taken to the advertiser's website. The placement of the ad is determined by the

keywords or search terms used. The more traffic a keyword brings, the higher the cost per click.

The two basic methods for advertising online are classified ads and banner ads. However, there are many other more costly options available, such as pop-up ads, pop-under ads, floating ads, etc.

For those with a limited budget and not enough time to consistently monitor their advertising campaigns, here are three more options to consider:

1. *E-zine or E-mail Advertising.* When someone "opts-in" to be on an e-mail list, he is interested in receiving information about a specific topic such as earning online, parenting, or golf. Find an e-zine or e-mail newsletter that has a loyal subscriber base that matches your target audience and place an ad in that publication. It is also possible to buy a special advertiser mailing to that list. Sending out e-mail promotions to people who have not requested your information is called "spam" and is not an acceptable practice.
2. *Free Classified Ads.* Most of the free classified ad websites are a waste of time. Although, one that is worth your effort is Craigslist (www.craigslist.org). Millions of people use Craigslist, but there is a catch: Craigslist is organized by geographical location. You have to choose one for each of your ads and cross-promotion is not allowed. Craigslist strives to have unique and continuously updated content. They will flag and delete your ad unless it is unique and relevant to its readers' interests. This means that you should choose the correct section for your ad and change your ad often. Post in a different city each day.
3. *Affiliate Marketing.* While this can be a little complicated to set up, affiliate marketing can be a very interesting choice for advertising your products. You create the ads and other marketing tools and website owners place them on their websites for free. If a sale is made as a result of one of those ads, you pay a previously agreed upon percentage of the sale.

Advertising Over the Air

Advertising on radio and television can be expensive and out of the reach of a start-up mail order business; however, there are ways to get on the air that can make it more affordable. In most cases, buying time locally will be the way to begin.

Radio

Every radio station has a specific format and can tell you who its listeners are. One of the most successful radio campaigns has been a mail order teddy bear company that advertises on stations listened to by men. The company offers to take the problems out of buying a great gift for all holidays—all the customer has to do is pick up the telephone. They dress the bears to customer specifications and deliver overnight. What more could a busy man ask for?

In radio, repetition is more important than in any other medium. You need to repeat your message several times during the commercial, and repeat the same commercial often. To supplement the time you purchase, you can offer some of your products as prizes in your station's contests or sponsor the traffic report so that your name is repeated frequently. You can ask the station to tell you when it has unsold time available, which they usually offer at a significantly reduced rate. In fact, many stations are used to giving price breaks to advertisers, so don't hesitate to ask for a bonus spot when you buy time.

Listen to the station you are considering and pay special attention to the commercials that run frequently. These advertisers are getting response. But if you don't hear mail order advertisers, maybe you should consider another venue. Don't be a pioneer when so much money is at stake.

If you decide to advertise, it is best to consult a professional to help you produce your spot; however, keep in mind the following points:

- Repeat your product name and your telephone number throughout the commercial.
- Don't be humorous unless it emphasizes your message. It can be distracting.
- Your sentences should be simple and easy to pronounce. Test your message before you use it on the air to make sure it can be understood.
- Your website address should be included and read as "Your Company dot com". Leave off the "http://www." for it is now understood.

Trying TV

Cable TV and other local stations can be affordable, but you have to be committed to repetition here too. Television time is sold by the second. No matter how low the "per second" fee is, don't forget what you've learned about targeting your market. It makes no sense to send messages out into the airwaves when your potential customer is not paying attention.

As in every other advertising opportunity, watch the stations you are considering. What commercials are repeated often? Are they for mail order products? If the station is not being used to sell by mail order, don't be the first to test the waters.

There is nothing worse than an unprofessional commercial on TV, and it will reflect badly on your product. Get help producing your spot, and keep the following tips in mind:

- Make sure your commercial can be understood, even with the sound turned off. The viewer needs to see your message.
- Include a call to action. An ordering telephone number and address should be shown in writing on the screen.
- An entertaining spot is okay and will even help the audience remember it; however, don't sacrifice time from your message.
- Show your website address on the ordering screen.

Free TV

Home shopping is a $100 billion industry. If you manufacture your own products, and one is offered for sale on QVC, Home Shopping Network, or a local clone, your business could literally be an overnight success. There is only one thing standing in your way: competition. And lots of it. Home Shopping Network has very strict quality and shipping requirements but will deal with small companies that have limited quantities. If you are serious about trying to promote via the home shopping route, you have to do your research. And remember the following points:

- Your product should be unique. They won't even consider a product that is readily available.
- Emphasize the value. Fine fabric, real gold, and so on, at a good price will capture attention.
- Make a video of yourself demonstrating your product. If you can convey a special quality, you will capture the attention of the buyers. You can also post the video on www.YouTube.com to help generate interest in your product.

Dos and Don'ts for Powerful Promotions and Ads

To help keep you focused, remember the following when you are ready to launch your campaign.

1. *Don't* neglect your research. Study the ads and promotional materials for products similar to yours. Make sure that there really is a waiting audience for your product.
2. *Don't* reinvent the wheel. All the research into what works and doesn't work has been done for you. Follow the proven principles, add a dash of your own creativity, and you are in business.
3. *Don't* keep 'em guessing. A creative ad can be interesting or eye-catching, but you must let your audience know exactly what you are selling. Don't sacrifice information for innovation.
4. *Do* emphasize your product's benefits. Details are important, but save them for the small print. People don't buy products. They buy answers to their problems, the chance for love and happiness, beauty, more time, fun, and ways to make more money. Emphasize your product's ultimate benefits to the consumer and you will attract attention.
5. *Do* remember eye appeal. Words are wonderful (and extremely important) but if your ad or other promotional material doesn't look good, the words may never be read.
6. *Do* ask for what you want. No matter how low-key your sales message is, tell the audience what they should do to respond. Use phrases such as "subscribe now," "mail the coupon today," "call now!," "click here," and "don't delay!"

Hitting the Jackpot: Free Publicity

There aren't many things in this world that are free. But there really is a way to promote your home-based mail order business and receive thousands of dollars worth of space in publications and time on radio and television at no real cost to you. It is called publicity. When you know what to say and how to attract the attention of the media, you can be one of the lucky business owners who receives this type of priceless attention.

Free publicity saves advertising dollars, but that's not the best part. Publicity almost always has a greater impact on the public than paid advertising ever could. Consumers can have some doubt when they read advertising claims, but editorial coverage means instant credibility for your business. When your potential customer reads about you in the morning paper or watches you on TV, you are delivering a message that comes with a built-in endorsement of the media outlet.

Publicity can make or break your business. The good points are obvious. Inquiries about your business and orders for your products come in quantities never before experienced. But like everything good, there can be a downside. Once your information is in the hands of the media, you lose all control over what is said. They can use small segments of your material and slant their coverage to fit their needs or the story being written. You can never guarantee that your complete story will be used or that information about how to contact you will be included. You also might be caught unprepared. If you cannot fill the orders or respond to the large number of requests for information, you could leave a disappointing impression. Sound scary? It is, but seeking publicity can also be profitable and worth every bit of trouble you might encounter.

There are many ways to get free publicity for your business, but each method has one common requirement: newsworthiness. You won't get on national TV, a website, or even in your local shopper's newspaper just because it's what you want. Editors have to fill the pages of their publications with interesting, educational, and informative material. Radio and TV producers have the same awesome responsibility. Each day they pick their topics from the wide variety of material that comes in the mail or over the wire services. Your press release or publicity kit will have just a few seconds to prove valuable, or it will land in the wastebasket. You need a "hook" to make your story interesting.

Winning Strategies

Large companies pay big fees to public relations firms to develop their press materials. If you can find a way to stand out within your chosen field, you can garner the attention of the press. And, you can do it all yourself at a fraction of the cost. Planning a publicity kit is a lot like creating a winning baseball team: Before you can score, you have to learn the rules of the game, and you have to use players who can make it in the big league. Your team is contained inside your media kit.

Your Publicity Team Lineup

First Base: A fact sheet describing your business and your qualifications.

Second Base: Descriptive material, including your brochure and product description, and possibly a sample of your product.

Shortstop: Photographs of you and/or your product.

Third Base: Copies of articles already published about you and your company, endorsements from your clients, and ideas for future stories.

Star Pitcher: Your press release, written in a format expected by editors and producers.

Outfield: Each component placed inside an attractive folder with a slot inside for your business card. A personal letter to each editor or producer can be attached to the outside of the folder.

Catcher: The carefully chosen media on your publicity list.

Because it can tell your story without additional help, your press release is the most important member of your team. In fact, sometimes it is beneficial to send your press release alone and let the editor or producer request additional information. It can be difficult to wade through an entire folder of information, trying to decipher the main message, so your kit could be culled out just because too much information has been given. You use an interesting press release to attract attention and then follow up with a full publicity kit—a home run—when more information is requested.

To be taken seriously, a press release must follow a traditional format. It is written in the form of a news story and speaks directly to the intended audience, not to the editor or producer to whom you are mailing it. And remember, the contents must be newsworthy, so you must describe how your business is new or different, or relate an important fact or a unique way of solving a problem.

A press release is always typed, double-spaced, and it is wise to limit the length to one or two pages. Smaller publications often run a press release exactly as written, whereas larger publications will edit it or extract bits of information to use in one of their articles. You can use your business letterhead or a plain piece of paper with your company's name typed at the top. This gives an easy reference point for your company's name, address, telephone and fax numbers, and Web and e-mail addresses. Then construct the release to include the following elements:

Contact Name. The name and telephone number of the person who is prepared to answer questions from the media should be placed in the upper left-hand corner of the page. Include this information even if it is printed in your letterhead.

Release Date. Most press releases include the line "For Immediate Release." However, if there is a reason for the media to delay using your material until a future date, you can use that date instead.

Headline. The headline is written in all capital letters and is centered. Choose your headline carefully, for if it is uninteresting, the rest of the release might not be read. For example, a mail order business might announce: NEW PRODUCT ADDED TO THE CLEANUP CATALOG. This type of headline would not attract as much attention as: SPEND LESS TIME ON HOUSEWORK: PROFESSIONAL OFFERS EFFICIENCY TIPS. Which headline would you use if you were an editor?

Lead Paragraph. The first paragraph of your press release should read like the lead of a newspaper story. Information is presented in descending order of importance, so your lead paragraph should explain the headline and contain the most important information in your story. An interesting quote or provocative statement can be effective. (Don't be afraid to quote yourself—*you* are the expert here!)

Body. The rest of the release fills in the details. It is always helpful to offer tips or other information that can be used by the reader. Keep your information concise and easy to understand. If the topic is too detailed, offer a free fact sheet, newsletter, or booklet, which will encourage the reader to contact you and will help you build a mailing list. When offering such printed material, be sure to include a sample for the editor's inspection.

Conclusion. This is the most important part. Include all of your contact information just as you would want to see it in print; for example, "To receive a free copy of the Cleanup Catalog, call 1-800-555-1234."

If your release is more than one page, write "—MORE—" at the bottom of the first page, and then put a part of the headline and page number at the top of the second page. At the end of the release type "###" or "—END—." Include an "Editor's Note" to give important information for the editor that is not included in the body, such as a list of items enclosed or availability for interviews.

Remember, everything about your press release and the envelope it arrives in "talks" to the reader. The paper should be of good quality, and there should be no spelling, punctuation, or grammatical mistakes. These types of errors can make a media person doubt your abilities and ignore your release.

Distributing Your Press Release Online

There are many newswire services that will make your press release available online. This is a viable addition to your public relations campaign if you have a website that readers can go to after reading your release. Although your press release is written for the media, it can also be picked up by Google and Yahoo and other search engines, so make sure your release will be appreciated by your target audience too. You can choose to e-mail your press release to specific media outlets. This will

Mothers' Home Business Network

P.O. Box 423

East Meadow, NY 11554

CONTACT: Georganne Fiumara

Georganne@HomeWorkingMom.com

FOR IMMEDIATE RELEASE

FREE E-BOOK HELPS MOMS FIND WORK-AT-HOME JOBS

To celebrate twenty-five years of helping moms earn money at home, Mothers' Home Business Network is giving away a free e-book titled, *Work-at-Home Job Finder for Moms*. It can be downloaded on their website, www.HomeWorkingMom.com.

Twenty-five years ago, mothers didn't have many work/family options. They either chose to stay at home with their children or they went to work and left them for eight hours a day. The Mommy Wars began as mothers in each group defended their choice. It was in that time and place that one mom decided there was a third option: Working at home.

"It is important for moms to be informed about potential scams and misleading opportunities," explains Georganne Fiumara, founder of

Mothers' Home Business Network and its website, HomeWorkingMom .com. "That's why we created a free guide that contains on-target information and pre-approved resources."

New moms are particularly vulnerable to work-at-home scams because they are driven by their desire to stay at home with their baby and have a limited amount of time to earn the money they need.

Work-at-Home Job Finder for Moms details the most common scams and misleading opportunities and gives all the information a mom needs to find legitimate at-home employment. You will learn how to use your talents to find real home employment and use freelance and telecommuting options to create at-home income. You will also learn how to prepare an online resume. The last chapter of *Work-at-Home Job Finder for Moms* encourages you to create your own opportunity by starting a home business.

"The Internet has increased a mom's legitimate opportunities and working at home is now a viable option that millions of mothers use," explains Ms. Fiumara. "Mothers today are so much more sophisticated than they were twenty-five years ago." Options for working at home and online include becoming a virtual assistant, an affiliate marketer, a content writer, a digital photographer, or a website designer.

To download your free copy of *Work-at-Home Job Finder for Moms*, go to www.HomeWorkingMom.com and click on the e-book cover in the upper right-hand corner of the home page.

END

require research on each of the potential recipient's websites. Some newspapers, especially, will give the proper e-mail address to use for press release submission. Use that e-mail address and/or choose the e-mail address of a writer that specializes in your topic.

Media Match-ups

To give your press release maximum opportunity to be used, make sure that you send it only to the appropriate media outlets. You have already determined your target audience. Send your release to the publications they read and the television and radio shows they watch and listen to. Try to think and write like the editors whose attention you are trying to attract.

Your home-based mail order business has probably given you expert status with the media. If you sell educational toys, you can speak about the learning opportunities that playing brings to children. If you owned the previously mentioned (fictional) Cleanup Catalog, you can give expert opinions on the best ways to clean every room in the house. You get the idea. If you have any writing ability, this expert status can give you the credibility you need to write articles or publish a newsletter on your topic.

To illustrate this point and emphasize the potential power of publicity, I will tell you an interesting story that took place in 1996. But first, a little background. For more than twenty years, I have been responsible for promoting Mothers' Home Business Network. We try to keep our membership fees affordable, so there isn't much of an advertising budget. We have had an excellent record of placing publicity, which has helped us become a large national organization. I have also written many articles about home business and usually receive some sort of mention for MHBN at the end of each article. If MHBN stopped operating today, we would get letters—lots and lots of letters—for many years, because of past publicity and references that appear in books still in print.

Since MHBN is an organization that provides information for mothers who want to work at home, young women with infants are a large percentage of our target audience. Throughout the years, I have written articles about home business for a new parent publication. This publication is targeted to the young mothers we want to reach. We have always received an enthusiastic response. This time, they published a short piece to help mothers who want to work at home detect possible work-at-home scams. I was quoted as the "expert" giving tips, and at the end of this piece, MHBN offered a free fact sheet titled *The Best Mother-to-Mother Home*

Business Opportunities and a brochure about joining the organization. We have received more than 15,000 requests for this free fact sheet.

Each respondent sent a self-addressed, stamped envelope so we did not have to address envelopes or pay for postage. Our only expense was the cost of the fact sheets and brochures, which was more than covered by the resulting memberships. Because all of these names were put in our computer, we also added many new names to our "house" list. Since these women are interested in the information we provide, they will be happy to receive any subsequent mailings we may send out. Focusing on the publications read by our target audience and providing valuable information and a free fact sheet were certainly effective that time. The potential power of publicity is awesome. And it can be yours if you follow the rules of the game.

Fifty Success Strategies for Mail Order Marketing

1. *Be persistent.* Persistence is the most valuable trait a marketer can have. Develop a marketing plan, and then work that plan consistently. Promote your business at least one day each week. Write letters to important contacts, send press releases, and, most of all, believe in your message. Marketing can take time. If you persist, you will eventually attract the attention you want and need.
2. *Set up a telephone tip line.* All you need is a dedicated telephone line and voice mail or an answering machine that will allow you to record daily or weekly tips related to the products you sell. This does not have to be a toll-free or 900 number line. At the end of the message, you can offer your catalog or further information about your business. A press release telling about the free tip line will help publicize your business.
3. *Read.* Read daily newspapers and current bestsellers to search for any tie-ins for your products. Then write a letter to the editor or the principals involved about how your product or business is relevant to their topic. Devise a press release that demonstrates how newsworthy your business is.
4. *Celebrate.* There are days, weeks, months, and years devoted to observing many different special events. Consult *Chase's Annual Events* (available at your local library) for a complete listing. A catalog of safety equipment for infants could be promoted in conjunction with National Baby Week. Products for fathers could be tied in with Father's Day.

5. *Measure your marketing.* Some of your marketing methods will be successful and others will be duds. You won't know which methods are winners unless you keep records of response.
6. *Don't worry about your competition.* In fact, make these potential enemies your friends. Joint marketing ventures as well as professional alliances can help boost your business. If your market is too saturated with competitors, try to find a niche that is being ignored.
7. *Be a big fish.* When you find a niche market, specialize in that area. It can help you to become an expert in your field. In other words, it is better to be a big fish in a little pond than a little fish in a big pond.
8. *Know your limits.* Do the work you are good at and farm out the rest to professionals. If you are terrible with numbers, hire an accountant. If you can't write, hire a copywriter. The expense will pay off in the long run.
9. *Know your target.* You can have the best products in your market and a knock'em dead catalog, but if you mail it to a disinterested person, you won't make a sale. The mailing lists you use should represent your target market.
10. *Mail to your customers first.* A mailing to your customer list should generate three to five times greater response than a list of prospects who did not request your information.
11. *Deliver without delay.* Those ordering through the mail want instant response and are usually willing to pay more to get it faster.
12. *Make responding easy.* Your telephone number and address should be easy to find. Your products should be pictured, and the descriptions should be easy to understand. Give your customers choices so that they can respond in the way that is comfortable for them.
13. *Survey savvy.* To learn exactly what your customers really want and need, ask them. Send a survey or questionnaire designed to find out what motivates them to buy. A promised discount or gift for answering could increase survey response and generate new business. Posting surveys online can help attract visitors to your website.
14. *Say "Happy Birthday."* Mail birthday greetings to your customers (you found out their birth dates on the survey you sent). Send a coupon as a birthday present or tell them they should treat themselves to your product to celebrate the event. If birthday marketing works for your customers, you can

expand your birthday-promotion mailings to include names on mailing lists that can be selected by birth date.

15. *Repeat, repeat, and repeat.* You can't present your message to your customers too many times. Repetition is the only way to keep information about your business in the minds and hearts of your target audience. Research shows that a message must be repeated to be remembered. Don't do one mailing. Do multiple mailings to the same people.
16. *Don't advertise.* Not unless you can choose a medium that allows you to repeat your ads. One-shot ads just don't work.
17. *Test by telephone.* Test a new promotional idea before you begin to use it on a wide scale by using your telephone instead of the mail. Experts say the response from one hundred telephone calls will be as accurate an indicator as the response from 1,000 pieces of mail. Testing by telephone will give you faster results, may cost less, and gives you the opportunity to receive additional input from those you survey. In a local market, you can also follow up a mailing with a telephone call to your potential customers.
18. *Raise your prices.* Believe it or not, you might make more sales by charging more. A higher price separates you from the crowd and implies that your product is better and deserves a premium price.
19. *Tag along with a trend or a current event.* Is your product environmentally friendly? Could it be related to the presidential campaign or the World Series? If you can position your products to fit in with a current event, you will gain credibility and interest by association.
20. *Face your customers.* Even though you operate through the mail, your customers like to see the face behind the business. Use your photo or those of staff members who will be taking calls in your promotional materials and on your website. A quote from those pictured can convey friendliness and build confidence.
21. *Toss a hot potato.* Make sure that you put a time limit on any promotional offer. Deadlines will increase responses by a certain date and your overall responses for any promotion. Give a believable reason for the deadline.
22. *Scare up some business.* If your product is necessary but not very appealing, scare your customers into action. Fear can motivate as well as pleasure and could be effective if your product can increase security, safety, or health. Make sure that you describe the dire consequences of not using your product.

23. *Write a letter to the editor and/or post comments online.* Local or national publications covering topics related to your business might be interested in your opinion. Your name, business name, and your location will be published if your letter is used, and you will help increase the public's perception of you as an expert in your field. Post comments online where permitted and include your website in your response.
24. *Choose advertising that lasts.* If you have a limited advertising budget, use your advertising dollars for ads that last for months, not minutes. Spend your dollars on an ad in the Yellow Pages or other directories, buy a magnetic sign for the side of your car, distribute clever bumper stickers, or give away T-shirts imprinted with your message.
25. *Give your sales force a makeover.* No, not your employees. I am talking about the paper promotional tools that represent your business. Your business cards, stationery, sales brochures, and product packaging should speak with one clear and cohesive voice. Quality paper, consistent typefaces, and a professionally designed logo will permit all your sales materials to properly represent your business.
26. *Turn your business card into a brochure.* Use the wasted space on the back of your business card to list your products or for an eye-catching photograph or illustration. Or choose a fold-over card to have even more promotional space.
27. *Always say thank you.* Thank your customers with a special offer. Thank anyone who refers business to you with a phone call, flowers, dinner, or a 5 percent commission. Thank your reliable suppliers with a letter and increased orders. They all will remember your kindness and want to help you again in the future.
28. *Give your products away.* Donating products to charitable or newsworthy causes can help you get in the papers, especially if you notify the media yourself.
29. *Learn from the winners.* There are very few original ideas in this world. If there is a company that you admire, analyze its marketing strategies and adapt them, improve them, make them your own. Use what works and don't reinvent the wheel.
30. *Give a gift.* If you don't give your customers a reason to respond to your promotional offers right away, they might forget. Offer a specialty item that is useful enough to save and will serve as a reminder of your business. For

example, a catalog of baby clothing could offer a free baby-proofing guide with each purchase. A notepad or a magnet imprinted with your business name will be saved and used.

31. *Promote with postcards.* First-class postage for a postcard is less than a letter. Postcards can convey a sense of urgency. If you print "Address Correction Requested" on the card, the post office will not charge for sending you the new addresses of your customers when the card is returned. This is an inexpensive way to update your mailing list. When your message is on a postcard, it is out in the open where everyone can see it. Not a bad deal.
32. *Encourage bounce-backs.* Enclose promotional material—one page or more—with your product shipments. If the customer is happy with his or her order, it is likely that you will attract another order. Or your customer might pass it on to a friend.
33. *Offer testimonials.* When your customers write you compliments, ask for permission to quote them. Be sure to use their complete names and their cities so your customers will know that these are real quotes.
34. *Give some options.* If you offer your customers the chance to choose between two or more options (usually discounts for multiple sales), they may concentrate on making that choice instead of deciding whether to accept or reject your offer.
35. *Use stamps.* When sending direct-mail promotions, use stamps instead of metered mail. It is more personal, and your letter will have an increased chance of being opened.
36. *Treasure technology.* By embracing all of the electronic ways to communicate with your customers, you can reach out locally, nationally, or internationally without leaving home.
37. *Ask for the sale.* This simple concept is often overlooked in mail order promotions, and the result is lower response.
38. *Publish a newsletter.* Newsletters can combine information with your sales message. Newsletters have an excellent chance of being read, and that is the first step to making a sale. Keep the newsletter short, publish frequently, and mail it to your house list. Repetition will make your message more memorable.
39. *Remember the key.* Every ad, every order form, every publicity effort should have a code contained in the address. If your ad appears in the magazine, *Popular*

Mechanics (a good place for classified advertising), the address could say, "Dep't PM," so that you will know before you open the letter that it is from that ad. Unless you know where your orders and inquiries are coming from, you will not know which marketing efforts to repeat and which to eliminate.

40. *Inspire confidence.* Studies report that confidence is the number-one reason why people choose to buy from a company. A commitment to customer service will help you keep the customers you have and attract new ones.
41. *Offer free information.* Every product user would be interested in receiving some free, related information. Publish a fact sheet or a booklet and offer it for free in your public relations and advertising. The respondents are potential customers and candidates for your house mailing list.
42. *Help save time and trouble.* People will buy products and use services that will make them feel safer, give them more free time, and take the tension out of their lives.
43. *Forget "I" and "we."* Instead, always say "you." Write all of your promotional materials from your prospect's point of view.
44. *Give your customers a break.* Send a 10 percent coupon along with your orders that expires within two weeks. If they are happy with their purchases, your customers will look for a reason to use the coupon.
45. *Keep it plain.* Many books will advise you to put a sales message on the outside of your envelope to arouse interest. This is not necessarily a good idea. Sometimes it is better to make your envelope appear to be a personal letter or give no clue to its contents. The recipient will then open it out of curiosity.
46. *Ask for referrals.* Offer your customers an incentive for giving you the names and addresses of friends and associates who may be interested in receiving your promotional materials.
47. *Offer a thirty-day, money-back guarantee.* Ordering by mail can be upsetting if the product ordered does not live up to expectations. Telling your customers that they can return the product in good condition to get their money back could give an extra incentive to place an order.
48. *Learn the Three Cs.* To succeed, a marketing plan requires commitment, consistency, and confidence. Once your plan is in place, you must be prepared to go with it, no matter what happens. Like planting a seed, your plan needs to be nurtured and given time to develop. Have confidence, and someday you will see your business blossom.

49. *Don't try to make money.* Instead, offer a useful product or service and make yourself and your customers happy. Remember the old adage, "Do what you love and the money will follow." It really works.
50. *P.S.* Always put a "P.S." at the end of your sales letters (even e-mail messages) detailing an important selling point. It is the first part of the letter that most people read.

Common Mail Order Marketing Questions

Q: There are infomercials on TV selling mail order business opportunities. These ads suggest placing one small classified ad that makes a profit and then taking out the same ad in more publications to multiply the profit. Is this realistic?

A: Yes . . . and no. It is difficult to sell products in general-interest publications such as daily newspapers. If you have chosen a product with a target audience in mind, you need to place your classified ads in the special interest publications that are read by those people. For example, if you have a product of interest to parents, you will want to advertise in parenting publications. If you place a classified ad in a parenting publication that is successful, it makes sense to place the same ad in similar publications and expect an equally good response.

Q: Advertising is so expensive. How can I be reasonably sure that an ad will be worth the money I invest?

A: There can be no guarantees when it comes to advertising; however, there are guidelines that you can follow to help minimize your risk. Understand why you are placing an ad and choose publications read by your target audience. Create an advertising budget and don't exceed it. Test your advertising concept on a small scale before buying more expensive ads. Estimate the number of responses you will receive, and figure out if these will be enough to break even. (An excellent response would be one-tenth of 1 percent of the readership.) Expand on the ads that work, and gradually eliminate the ones that do not generate enough income.

Q: Can a small company really get free publicity in national magazines or on TV? Won't I be wasting my time?

A: Never underestimate the possibilities of free publicity. Company size does not matter if you can present an editor or a producer with an interesting or newsworthy angle to even the most common products. By sending out a press release, Mothers' Home Business Network received publicity in the *Detroit Free Press* before we were even operational. We were listed as a resource after an article about working at home. For the first few months, almost all of our members came from Detroit! In fact, three days after mailing our first press release, our telephone began ringing, and a variety of national publications eventually used our story. Examine the publications, and view the shows you are targeting. What kinds of stories do they use? Copy the same format, and you could become a media star!

06 Mail Order Marketing Tools

You might feel a little intimidated by all of the marketing methods that are available to direct marketers today. But it is a mistake to feel that way. As a home-based mail order business owner, you have more to gain by embracing technology than do the large corporations. Computers, fax machines, modems, and all the other telecommunications advances have made it possible for home-based businesses to compete with the big guys. They allow us to produce work and communicate information on an equal level.

Have you ever heard the old adage "The more things change, the more they stay the same"? Strip away all of the hype, and you will see that electronic marketing can be as comfortable and familiar as any other marketing method. Both traditional and electronic marketing share one goal: to elicit a response from an individual. The good news is that even if you can't set the clock on your VCR, you can learn to communicate electronically. It does not have to be a do-it-yourself proposition.

Will letters and direct-mail promotions disappear in the twenty-first century? Not likely. Even though mail volume has not grown as much as predicted over the past few years, the mail will always be used as a promotional tool. Most successful marketers, however, no longer limit their marketing to the mail.

Here are just a few reasons why you should learn how to enhance your direct-mail promotions with more advanced marketing techniques:

- They will help you maximize your sales, because you will be able to reach more members of your target audience at once and without delay.

- Database marketing will help you learn more about each individual customer, allowing you to customize your message and satisfy specific needs (and make more sales).
- Technology is interactive. You will be able to have an ongoing dialogue with your customers. You can speak *with* them instead of at them and develop a relationship.
- When you make it easier (and more fun) for your customers to spend money, your profits will increase.
- Your sales ability can be enhanced without hiring employees.
- You can satisfy your customers' need for speed. Point, click, and they are yours.
- Technology helps smaller businesses outshine larger but less advanced companies.
- Your customers will perceive that your company is on the cutting edge.

The Future Is Yours

For just a moment forget about marketing with technology and think about the reason why you decided to work at home. Chances are you wanted to be in charge of your days, to be more available to your family, and work the hours you choose. Now imagine how much freedom you could have if you could literally put your office in a briefcase. If you have a laptop computer, wireless Internet, and a cell phone, you can do business anywhere. Those commercials you see on TV showing people working on the beach are not science fiction. That kind of lifestyle is possible to you right now. Or maybe you don't want to have a virtual office. You just want to be able to get away from your home once in a while. Put voice mail on your telephone, pack your cell phone, and you can go anywhere while staying in touch with your business twenty-four-hours-a-day, seven-days-a-week.

Instant communication has become part of everyone's life. Children as young as the age of 10 have cell phones so that their friends (and parents) can reach them immediately, no matter where they are. These young people have always had the Internet and e-mail in their lives. In a few years, these children of technology could be your customers. Do you think that they will be willing to wait for information about your products? If your company doesn't provide instant communication—and gratification—they will find one that does.

The electronic marketing choices you make will ultimately depend on the price range of the products you are selling, your marketing budget, and the ordering preferences of your target market. Not all of the marketing methods described in this chapter are high tech. Many involve the telephone or telephone line, and some are actually familiar to you right now.

This is the dawn of a new age. If you grow with these trends, you won't be left behind when tomorrow comes. If you use traditional direct-marketing methods and add-in online marketing, you will be ready for unlimited success.

E-mail Marketing

E-mail is a very unique form of marketing. The cost is low—very low. And it can be extremely effective. But those marketing by e-mail need to learn and follow the rules. Indiscriminate e-mailing can actually have a destructive effect on your business. While there are plenty of businesses doing untargeted and unsolicited bulk e-mail mailings and some are even making money, this is not the way to go. Called spamming, mass e-mailings could elicit sales but can also get you into trouble. Most Internet service providers will discontinue your account if they receive complaints that you are sending bulk e-mail. The Can Spam Act of 2003 requires e-mail marketers to follow specific rules. Go to www.fcc.gov/cgb/consumerfacts/canspam.html for guidelines. There are many ways for you to market your website and your business via e-mail and receive enthusiastic responses from the recipients.

One-to-one e-mail can be one of the most effective and far-reaching marketing methods available to you. The informal nature and immediacy of e-mail makes it possible for you to develop valuable relationships with your customers and the visitors who write to you. Answer questions, make inquiries, share information, and soon you will have a loyal customer. Writing an e-mail, however, is a little different from writing a letter.

E-mail should be short and to the point. Break your message into small paragraphs of only three to six lines, and leave a space between paragraphs. If a lot of information must be included, use headings to separate your points. Do not attach files with your e-mail messages unless you have arranged to do so in advance. Most people hesitate to download files from people they do not know, and often the recipient will not have the ability to open the file. Instead, put all of the information into the e-mail and post graphics on a Web page. Be sure to include the URL in the e-mail.

There are opt-in e-mail lists available. These contain the names of people who have indicated that they would like to receive information about certain topics. You can rent an opt-in e-mail list, but you must be careful. Some of the people on some of these lists did not actually opt in; they just did not opt out when given the choice. Make sure that you ask how the names were gathered before renting a list. Since e-mail costs so much less than traditional direct mail, you can try this method of promotion and see what happens. Directing recipients to your website can be much more effective than trying to sell a product in the e-mail itself.

Toll-Free Telephone Numbers

In the 1970s there were a few pioneering marketers who offered toll-free numbers to their customers. Back then telephone rates were high, and limited services were available. Today the use of toll-free numbers has escalated to the point that new toll-free exchanges had to be introduced. The supply of new 800 numbers expired, and now 888, 877, and 866 also are toll-free exchanges. Note, however, that a 2002 study by Radio Recall revealed that 95 percent of consumers recognized the 800 exchange, but only 18 percent knew 866 was also toll-free.

A survey by Matrixx Marketing showed that consumers like using a toll-free telephone number to order or get information about a product. Why do they feel that way? It is obvious that they like saving money with the free call, even though the higher the income level of the respondents, the more frequent the use of toll-free numbers. In fact, 64 percent of those calling toll-free numbers have an income at or above $40,000. Why do they call? Studies reveal that 71 percent said it was to get information, 23 percent wanted to ask a specific question, and 66 percent stated that operator knowledge, courtesy, and helpfulness were absolutely essential.

Should you offer a toll-free calling option to your customers? Although there are some exceptions, you probably should offer this option. One national marketer I know sells a service priced at $3,000 and does not offer a toll-free calling option. He feels that if his prospects are unwilling to pay for a telephone call, they will be unable or unwilling to pay for his services. There may be some logic to this way of thinking, but I do not agree. A toll-free telephone number is more than a free calling option. It shows your potential customers that you really want to hear from them, and it is a gesture of goodwill. According to AT&T, prospects are seven times more likely to call if they can use a toll-free number.

As a start-up company, you may understand the benefits of toll-free calling, but you might not be able to afford it or derive full benefit from it at first. Local toll-free numbers are affordable, but if you are marketing on a national level you will have to do your homework and compare rates carefully. Some companies charge monthly fees (some do not) and a per-minute charge. Flat per-minute rates or rates based on distance are also available. If you receive a large number of calls, your telephone bill could be a few thousand dollars per month.

Service bureaus that offer a toll-free telephone number and credit card processing can be a good choice for small businesses. Because of volume, they charge much lower rates, and you could find a good match; however, it is necessary to research the service bureau you want to use. Speak with existing clients and learn all you can about a company before signing on. A customer will judge your company by the way his or her call is handled by your service bureau. Before adding a toll-free calling option, consider the following questions:

- Is it cost-effective? As always, you must analyze the cost versus the potential benefits.
- Can you accept credit card orders? If not, the value of a toll-free telephone number is diminished.
- Do you have a way to answer your toll-free line twenty-four hours a day? If not, hours need to be specified when advertising your number.

Voice Mail

How would you like to throw out your answering machine and hire an assistant to help you answer your telephone? No more garbled messages, broken tapes, or equipment failure. Sound good? If you could hire an assistant, what qualities would you look for? Your assistant should be efficient, cheerful, tireless, and able to answer many calls, one call at a time. Impossible? Not if you use voice mail.

An AT&T study indicated that 75 percent of calls used to go unanswered. Voice mail changed that statistic. With voice mail, your calls will always be answered, and your callers will never hear a busy signal again. Voice mail in its most basic form is an automated service that acts much like an answering machine but with more options. In its more advanced form, it can route incoming calls to different departments or individual "mailboxes" where callers can listen to announcements, leave a message, or request that the person be paged.

You can buy voice mail equipment to use in your office, or you can use the service provided by your telephone company. There are benefits and disadvantages to each option. If you go with your telephone company, you can be sure that your telephone will always be answered, even when your line is busy. Voice mail subscribers call a special telephone number and key in a password to pick up messages and use the telephone keypad to skip, repeat, save, and so on. You have more opportunity to manipulate your messages than on an answering machine. There is a limit to the number of messages a telephone voice mail system can hold at one time. Your messages will be saved for up to one month. Most companies stutter the sound of the dial tone to let you know if you have a message. You are charged local rates for each call that comes in and each time you pick up your messages. These charges are in addition to a monthly fee of approximately $12 to $20 for a business line.

It will cost a minimum of $1,000 to $2,000 to set up a voice mail system that is run by a dedicated computer system in your office. You will be able to set up a more elaborate system, but doing so can be complicated and expensive. You are not limited to a set number of messages or a predetermined number of mailboxes. The technology is changing rapidly, however, and you could get stuck with expensive hardware that is outdated.

Your voice mail system should be easy to use. Keep the following tips in mind if you decide to use this technology:

- Make your greeting businesslike and to the point.
- Ask for details. Encourage your callers to give the reason for their call.
- Tell your callers how to skip your message. Most systems allow regular callers to press the pound sign (#) to accomplish this feat.
- Check for messages every time you finish a conversation.

Telemarketing

Speaking with your prospects by telephone can dramatically increase your response rate. There is nothing more personal than a one-on-one conversation. The public often has a poor perception of telemarketers. Many call during inconvenient times and often read from a script, without any true knowledge of the products or services they are selling. That type of telemarketing has no place in your business.

Most mail order businesses depend on inbound telemarketing, although there is a place for outbound telemarketing in your marketing plans, especially when it is combined with direct mail.

Inbound Telemarketing

Inbound telemarketing takes place when a customer wants to know more about your products or is ready to place an order. Some people prefer to use the mail to ask for information or place an order. But when you measure the response from those who call, it will always outperform mail-in response.

The person answering your telephone must be able to do more than passive order taking or recording of a name and address to send information. A list of questions should be used to elicit information about your callers. How did they find out about your business? What related products would interest them? Effective order taking can increase sales and help your company build a relationship with its customers at no additional cost to you.

To increase the calls coming in to your business use these tips:

- Make it easy for potential customers to reach you. Display your telephone number repeatedly on all of your promotional materials.
- Give your customers more reasons to call. Offer free information or a special discount on merchandise when ordering by phone.
- Consider using call-processing technology that will help you route your calls to the correct person or give automated information that your caller requests.

Outbound Telemarketing

There is one sure way to avoid problems with an outgoing telemarketing campaign. It is the same rule that we have been emphasizing throughout this book: Make sure that every single one of your prospects is a member of your target audience. How can you do that? Never make a call unless information in some form has been requested by the prospect or the prospect has been referred to you.

The very best way for a home-based mail order business owner to use outbound telemarketing is in conjunction with direct mail, especially with a big-ticket item. When a prospect requests information about your product, you can increase your sales dramatically by making a follow-up telephone call. It is the perfect combination

Hamilton East Public Library

of marketing techniques. But don't forget your basic training. The only way you will make the sale is if you ask for it.

Here are some other points to keep in mind when calling your customers:

- Be up front. Tell your prospect exactly why you are calling.
- Be prepared. Know what you want to say before you call. Anticipate objections and prepare your replies.
- Convey confidence. Speak clearly and with knowledge.
- Stay on the subject. Let your prospects talk as much as they want, but when you speak, stick to your point.
- Don't interrupt or rush your prospect. It will seem like you are not paying attention or that you don't have a genuine interest in what is being said.
- Know what main points you want to make, but don't read from a prepared script. Instead, discuss the product's benefits and be sincerely enthusiastic.

Before You Pick up the Phone . . .

The Federal Trade Commission (FTC) has issued guidelines to protect consumers from deceptive and abusive telemarketing practices. The Telemarketing Sales Rule enables the FTC to impose fines up to $11,000 for violations. Keep the following rules in mind when planning your telemarketing strategy:

- Outgoing sales calls may be placed between 8:00 a.m. and 9:00 p.m.
- You must identify yourself at the beginning of the call and tell what you are selling.
- If there is a prize promotion, you must state that there is no purchase necessary to win.
- You must give the odds of winning the prize.
- You must get written or taped authorization if money is to be taken from a consumer's bank account.
- You must disclose the total cost of what you are offering and any restrictions that apply before asking for credit information.
- If you have a no-refund policy, you must state so.
- You cannot operate schemes that penalize prior victims of telemarketing fraud by offering to get their money back.
- You cannot call people who have asked not to be called. For information about the National Do Not Call Registry, go to: www.donotcall.gov or www.ftc.gov.

Fax Marketing

Some experts predict that the fax machine will become outdated and unnecessary as e-mail and other emerging technologies replace it. Maybe. or maybe not. Fax technology is so cost-effective, dependable, and easy to use that it will be with us for many years to come. E-mail won't replace the U.S. Mail, and fax machines won't become obsolete anytime soon.

When you have the ability to exchange information quickly, you can save time and money by faxing. Besides the ability to transmit a page of information in seconds, there are two main ways fax machines are used for marketing purposes: fax-on-demand and fax broadcasting.

- *Fax-on-demand.* Customers call and request product information to be faxed to them. Documents can be electronically stored and faxed on request. Catalogs, especially business-to-business catalogs, often offer fax-on-demand for potential customers who require additional information about a product.

  When you order by mail, you can't touch the product you are considering. If I were in a computer store, I could turn the software box over and read all of the specifications. Fax-on-demand allows me to get as much information, if not more, before I buy.

  When customers call your fax-on-demand system, you will have a record of their name, fax number, and the type of information they have requested. You can use this information to create a database of names and fax further information to them in the future.
- *Fax broadcasting.* A personalized document that is sent to a large number of contacts, fax broadcasting is similar to doing a mass mailing but better. There are no papers to print, no envelopes to stuff, and no postage. Your message is delivered to all parties on the same day, and you don't have to pay for an overnight delivery. Best of all, it is automatic. Once it is set up, you push a button and the machine does all the work.

One important note: The FCC's Telephone Consumer Protection Act protects against unsolicited faxes that advertise a product or service. This law allows unhappy fax recipients to file suit for actual monetary loss or at least $500 in damages for each violation. The court is allowed to triple the award. Although it is unlikely that your fax recipients would take you to court, you don't want to waste time and money sending information to disinterested people. To avoid trouble you should get permission from everyone on your fax list. An alternative would be to put a telephone number on the fax that people can call to request that their names be taken off your list.

There are service bureaus that will handle fax-on-demand and fax broadcasting for you, or you can set up a fax system and do it yourself. Prices of fax systems that allow small businesses to handle their own fax-on-demand and fax broadcasting have dropped 50 percent but still require a substantial investment. In most cases a service bureau will be your best bet for fax-on-demand, because it can be costly to set up an automatic system. Fax broadcasting can be done from your office on a limited basis if your fax machine has that capability; however, if you want personalization, a service bureau might be preferable.

Faxing From Your Computer

If you already have a computer and printer, you may not need a stand-alone fax machine. Some computers come with a fax modem, or you can add one on and install fax software. This will give you the capability to fax any document that is in your computer and receive any document. You won't have to print out a document before you fax it; however, you also won't be able to fax a document unless it is in your computer, which could be inconvenient. Multi-function printer/fax/copy/scan machines may be the best choice.

To receive a fax through your computer modem, your computer must be turned on and in the fax-receive mode. Your fax modem will answer the call. Incoming faxes can be printed out or viewed on your computer. You have the ability to delete faxes you do not want to print. Fax software usually works in the background, so you can receive a fax while you are working on another project. Faxing this way gives you clearer images, but it requires a lot of disk space.

Database Marketing

The more you know about your customer, the more sales you will make. Database marketing helps you to identify the traits of your individual customers, and that gives you the ability to satisfy their needs.

Your computerized list of customers—their names and addresses—comprises your company's database. Database marketing happens when you gather as much data as possible about your customers, analyze it, and use it to build a closer relationship with them.

MCI's Friends and Family is a good example of database marketing. The company consulted with each of its customers individually and offered them a way to save money when speaking to their most-called family members and friends. By interacting individually with customers, MCI was able to make existing customers happy and gained new customers in the process.

If you keep good records, it will be easy to determine all of the basic information about your customers and the kinds of products they order. When you speak with your customers, use that opportunity to add information to your database. Determine what information will be the most useful and fashion some questions to elicit the right responses. Other ways to acquire information are customer questionnaires, membership forms, and product-registration cards. Every time you acquire any kind of information about your customers, enter it in your records.

Once you have the data, you need to analyze it. What do your customers have in common? Who are your best customers? What products do they buy?

Some possibilities for using your data will become apparent without much work. Say you sell children's books by mail. Your customer begins by buying books for new readers. If you track that customer, you will know what level of books the reader will be reading as the years progress. You will also know the age and gender of the child in question. What other products do you have that would be of interest to your young customer? When is his or her birthday? Send a card and a free book to celebrate, and you might just gain a customer for life.

Specialized computer software can help you determine some of the more complicated insights. Once you organize your customers into categories, you will be able to market to them on a more individualized basis. When you develop a relationship with the people who support your business, the result will be customer loyalty and increased sales.

To achieve maximum results from your database marketing efforts, here are some positive steps to take:

- Offer incentives. If you have loyal customers, keep them that way. Give them a reason to maintain their loyalty by offering discounts or premiums when a level of sales is reached. This concept has been extremely successful for airlines and their frequent-flier benefits.
- Track your customers' behavior. If they purchased a gift for holiday giving last year, remind them of the upcoming occasion in time for another sale.

- Predict your customers' needs. If they buy a coffeemaker, they will need new filters. If they buy a printer, they will need cartridges. Anticipate these needs and offer an easy way for them to make a purchase.

Common Mail Order Marketing Tool Questions

Q: If the traditional marketing methods work, why do I have to try new ways to promote my mail order products?

A: You don't have to do anything that makes you feel uncomfortable; in fact, don't ever change a marketing method that works. But the more traditional methods can be enhanced by the new technologies, and interest in these areas will grow in the immediate future. It always pays to have your finger on the pulse of future trends.

Q: Besides sending press releases, what would I use fax broadcasting for?

A: Fax broadcasting is most useful in business-to-business communications, because you cannot be sure that your customers have faxing capabilities. You could use fax broadcasting to announce special offers, give any sort of information update, or even produce a fax newsletter.

Q: How do I find the time to develop a relationship with my customers using database marketing, social networking, and telemarketing? I barely have the time to get my orders in the mail.

A: Recording information about your customers in your database is an ongoing activity. Do what you can to create a complete record of your customers' likes and dislikes. Social networking allows you to sell to "friends" you make online. The trust is implicit and you can't afford to ignore the possibilities. Even if you don't do formal telemarketing, use every conversation you have with your customers and potential customers to build a relationship. As your business grows, try to concentrate on the business-building aspects and let others do the more menial tasks.

07 Selling Your Products Online

In the history of mail order, there has been no innovation equal to the Internet. The statistics change daily, but at this writing *The World Fact Book* reports that there are more than 231 million Internet users in the United States. Forrester Research reports that in 2009 154 million people in the U.S. bought something online—that's 67 percent of the online population. They predict online retail will reach nearly $250 billion and account for 8 percent of total U.S. retail sales by 2014. But you should know that $917 billion worth of retail sales were "Web influenced" in 2009. Even though the Internet is growing at an astonishing rate, it is still in its infancy. Those who go online with their business now will still be one of the pioneers in the years to come. Opportunities abound, and those who take the time to learn the right way to approach this large and fast-growing audience will certainly be able to find success online.

Shopping Online versus Catalog Shopping

Mail order entrepreneurs need to know that shopping online is quickly overtaking catalog shopping. A study conducted by Greenfield Online of Westport, Connecticut, showed that while 38 percent of all consumers look at catalogs when considering a purchase, 30 percent go online to browse. Of these, 22 percent actually make catalog purchases, but 18 percent make their purchases online. Think about it: Why would a consumer send for a catalog if he or she could access a company's goods immediately on a personal computer?

Online success story Amazon.com is an excellent example of why buyers are flocking online to make their purchases. Amazon.com offers the visitor a selection of more than 2.5 million books. According to founder Jeff Bezos, if Amazon produced a catalog containing all of these books, it would be the size of forty New York City telephone books!

When you are shopping online, you don't have to get dressed, leave home, drive to the store, or find a parking space. The weather is not a factor, nor is time of day. As long as you have electricity in your home, you can shop online twenty-four hours a day, seven days a week. If you are looking for a specific book, you will find it on Amazon.com. It may not be in your local bookstore, which never stocks more than 175,000 titles, no matter how large it is. The same convenience factor applies to most other merchandise. Your favorite store may run out of your size in the sweater you want, but your online retailer will have every size available at its website.

Shopping online will never completely replace catalogs and retail stores, but it is clear that a large share of the money spent on goods and services will come from online sales, and that number will increase dramatically each year. If you want part of that action, this chapter will give you the inside information you need to make the right moves, right from the start.

Every Business Needs a Website

You can use your website as a public relations tool to promote an existing business, or you can set up a functioning store and sell your products online. No matter what level of commitment you make, if you are in business, you need to have an online presence.

Here are just a few of the reasons why your business needs a website:

- *It's accessible twenty-four hours a day.* Your website allows you to attract new customers, service the ones you have, make a good impression—and sales—all day long, even while you sleep.
- *It's personal and interactive.* Computers are located in people's homes, and they are very close to the screen while viewing your website. One-on-one communication with your customers is possible to achieve in this type of atmosphere.
- *It's a customer service assistant.* Your website can automatically answer basic customer service questions by listing frequently asked questions (FAQs) that visitors can access. Other questions can be asked and answered by e-mail, which can be more convenient than telephone calls. Provide your e-mail address and you will have created another way for customers to contact you.
- *It levels the playing field.* Your competition has a website—or soon will. Do you want them to get your share of the business? On the Web, you can

have a site that equals or surpasses the presentation of larger and better-financed companies.

- *It attracts new customers.* Those searching for your type of merchandise can discover your website and learn about your business for the first time while they are surfing the Web. Interested customers can go to your website to read information they need to help them make a buying decision.
- *It's a store.* You don't have to accept orders on your website for your business to benefit, but you can create a full-service store that will showcase all of your products. Your store can have shopping carts, accept credit card orders, and even have salespeople who can connect in real time and answer questions.
- *It's a communications center.* You can keep your customers or clients up to date about new products or services, special offers, and other important information. Customers can contact you via e-mail to give you instant feedback about your business or just ask a question.
- *It's a marketing and public relations tool.* When potential customers or media outlets want to know more about your business, you won't have to stop working and prepare a presentation kit or make a trip to the post office or overnight delivery service. All you have to do is refer them to your website and tell them what to look for. The free content on your site will also create goodwill in your customers and make a good impression on those evaluating your business. You can post your press releases in a special section of your site.
- *It's affordable.* A big budget will not guarantee an effective website. Just look at some of the websites of large corporations and you'll see what I mean. Your site can be as colorful, meaningful, and content-rich as the big guys'—without investing a lot of money.
- *It's your ticket to the future.* The sooner you take your business online, the sooner you will be able to say that you are positioned to take part in the future of mail order commerce.

This Way to the Web

The first step to bringing your business online is to become an Internet user yourself. Begin to use the Web for your own information needs and shopping. Explore websites in general and specifically in your field. Take note of what works and what doesn't work. What attracts your attention? What does it feel like to wait while a graphics-intensive page tries to load on your computer screen? Is it the bells and whistles that impress you, or are you drawn to sites with clean designs and valuable information? When you see websites you like, note which companies are responsible for the design, and visit their sites to see what they have to offer you.

Creating and Registering a Domain Name

When you build a website, you get to choose your own unique address. Your choice will be one of the most important decisions you make for your website. Also called a domain name or URL (Universal Resource Locator), your address should be simple, descriptive, and memorable. Many companies use their business name, and that can make it easier for customers to find you. If your business name is too long or uninteresting, your domain name can consist of any descriptive phrase or benefit you give your customers. All of the words in your domain name run together or can be separated by dots or dashes. Unless they have seen it in print, potential customers won't know how you've chosen to separate words; if they do not type in the address exactly as you have registered it, they will receive an error message or be taken to someone else's site. It is usually beneficial to run the words together.

When I took Mothers' Home Business Network online, I chose www.mhbn.com. As time passed, however, I realized that another name might be more memorable. Ultimately, I registered HomeWorkingMom.com. I liked the way that "mom" rhymed with ".com," and the name identified the exact person who could benefit from using the site. I pay a slight additional fee so that either address will take you to the same site, but the site is promoted under HomeWorkingMom.com. It would have been a lot easier and less expensive if I had taken more time to choose my website's address. You can learn from my mistake. Before you make your final choice, consider the following suggestions:

- Try your business name first. How does it look as one lowercase word (yourbusinessname.com)? Will potential customers be looking for you on the Web, or will you be trying to attract visitors who are interested in your topic and don't know your name? Can your business name be shortened and still be identifiable?

- Write down all of the words that convey the benefits your business offers. Would two or more of the words combined create an address that is easy to remember and easy to spell? Write down a few of your ideas and ask everyone you know which name they prefer.
- Investigate what URLs your competitors are using. Can you take the URL of an existing and successful site and use the same concept for your domain name?
- Once you have decided on one or two candidates, it is time to find out if those names have already been taken. You can do the search and registration yourself or you can pay your Web designer or server to do it for you. If you'd like to begin the search yourself, go to www.networksolutions.com. There you can type in your proposed name to see if it is already being used. If it is not, it might be prudent to register it as quickly as possible. If you want your URL to be your business name and someone else has already registered it, you can add the word "online" to your business name. For example, if your business name is XYZ and www.xyz.com has already been taken, you can try to register www.xyzonline.com.
- Most of the good names are being taken quickly so you might have to be a little creative. Before you register your choice, you must choose the company that will host your website; that information must be included in the registration.

Who Will Design Your Website?

Even the largest Web design companies do not always understand what it takes to create a site that is easy to navigate and presents your product in the best way. If you surf the Web, you will find that the sites of some large corporations are not much more than expensive electronic brochures.

I would suggest that any company starting from scratch with a limited budget should find an individual who designs and hosts websites. This person can become your friend, your guru, and your support system as you create your company's first website. To find the right person, visit lots of sites, especially in your area of interest, and note the designer/host of the sites you like the best. You can usually find this information on the bottom of the main page of the site.

PROFIT PROFILE: Angela Smith, Internet Helping Hand

Angela Smith has been online for more than twenty years. And throughout those years she has always offered an outstretched helping hand to those just coming online. She taught herself how to design websites using online tutorials (like the one at www.htmlgoodies.com); by networking and offering free advice, she has made lasting contacts and friends. "I first went online because it allowed me to communicate with people all over the U.S. and Canada, and today the Internet and the World Wide Web offer limitless possibilities. Being able to reach people and information all over the world with the touch of a button still amazes me," she explains.

Along the way, Angela has always put people first by simplifying the technology and never taking advantage of the inexperienced. She has designed many award-winning websites but today Web design is no longer her primary focus. Instead, she offers very reasonably priced website hosting and all of the services a website needs to maximize customer service. "I noticed that many small businesses were paying outrageous prices for a presence on the Web and decided to offer hosting and a package of services such as unlimited storage space, a Web control panel to make changes easier, a shopping cart, unlimited autoresponders, and much more for under $10 a month."

Knowing how important content is to the success of websites and e-zines, Angela has developed two sites offering free articles and columns that can be used as long as the author's name and contact information are given.

I found Angela Smith in an online discussion group about home business soon after I went online. I was trying to decide if I should try to build HomeWorkingMom.com myself or hire someone to do the work. My budget was small and I was unsure of my next step. Angela contacted me, intrigued by the idea of designing a site for Mothers' Home Business Network. Angela deserves so much of the credit for the great success of HomeWorkingMom.com. Since you may not be lucky enough to find her in a discussion group, you can e-mail her at angelabsmithaz@gmail.com.

Don't just choose the first person you contact. Instead, interview a few people and get complete details about the services they offer and the prices they charge. Ask for a list of the sites each person has designed and go check them out. Ultimately, you must choose a person who is not only talented but has a personality that fits with yours.

Do-It-Yourself Options

If you want or need to put up a website by yourself, there are some affordable and doable options available to you. Many people begin with a blog and expand from there. WordPress is a free blogging platform that can be adapted to look like a website. You could start a free, hosted blog at www.WordPress.com, but that is not what I recommend because you have very limited options and don't have control of your server. Instead, you need your own hosting account on a Web server and your own domain name. Some hosts offer auto-installation of WordPress, so you can check for that option to make things easier for you. You can register your domain name, find website hosting, and install WordPress automatically if you go to the website, www.WonderfulWebsiteStore.com

You have the option of keeping your website in a blog format, you can just put a blog on the site, or you can eliminate the blog feature altogether.

My website, HomeWorkingMom.com, is a WordPress website. I had a designer install and adapt the theme, but then I was able to learn how to add the articles and make changes myself. I love the look of a WordPress website and, even better, the independence it gives me to maintain it myself.

There are other do-it-yourself options that can help you create your own website or even just a Web page. You will find some of the best ones listed in the appendix of this book.

Building Your Website

Even if you have decided not to do the work yourself, you cannot sit back and leave the concept and content of your website to anyone else. Only you understand your business and only you can bring your special point of view to your website. Your business name is on it, so you must decide how it will look and what you want it to say. What will be the message of your site? What type of free information (content) can you provide? How do you want it to look? What will you do to involve your visitors?

You will go to a lot of trouble to bring visitors to your website. How long will they stay after their computer screen fills with your message? Remember, all it takes is just one click of the mouse and a potential customer could be gone, never to return. But if you make your website an inviting place to visit and give your visitors a good reason to stay a while and to return again and again, you will have happy customers and a successful online presence.

If you are creating a website for an existing business, you do not have to generate a lot of income online right away. Your original goal can be to attract attention and create goodwill. If you are starting a new business and your website is your only source of income, you would want to be ready to sell all of your wares from day one. Either way, there are essential elements that must be considered while you are creating your site.

Essential Elements for Every Website

What do you hope to accomplish with your website? Whom do you want to attract? Is your primary objective the sale of products? Or do you want to develop a national or international reputation for your company? Do you want to be entertaining or serious? Will customer service and lead generation be your main focus? Establishing specific goals will help plan an effective site.

A Plan

Good organization and planning will be the strong foundation that your website needs to succeed. Your opening page will make or break your site. Make sure the design, copy, and content relay how your site will benefit the readers and give them a reason not to click off. An attention-getting headline with an appealing graphic can be very effective. Your home page should also include a list of the other pages on your site, with links to each page.

You can begin your plan by writing down key words that describe your business and the information you want to provide. Plan a separate Web page for each of those words, then structure your site so that the information is as easy as possible to locate.

Design

Your pages must be designed with the visitor in mind. Although it may be tempting to fill your pages with animated graphics, background music, or talking clowns, these effects can take a long time to load and can even make older computers freeze. Slow loading = lost customers. Your page design should be colorful but clean and easy to read. Effective Web page design enhances your message and does not need to dazzle your visitors.

Once you have chosen a "look" for your pages, carry out that same theme throughout your site. This creates a feeling of continuity. Information will be the thing that attracts visitors to your website, but the design will help create a pleasant experience and encourage them to stay long enough to become customers.

Content

In the beginning, those using the Internet expected that they would be able to access free information. Asking for payment was a big turnoff. Although today's Web surfers will go shopping, they still appreciate and expect that they will get a lot of usable information for free. The free content of your website will provide a reason for visitors to come to your site and then give them a reason to return. They will come for the free stuff, but if they stick around long enough, your visitors may become your customers.

If your business involves the sale of tools, you could put how-to home improvement articles on your site. A baby clothing business could offer parenting articles. A bookseller could provide book reviews. You get the idea.

You can find free content on the Web (see Profit Profile: Angela Smith), or you can ask experts to write articles on your subject and "pay" them by providing a link to their websites or e-mail addresses. The more free and meaningful content you have on your site, the easier it will be to get free publicity and obtain links at other sites.

Including some content that changes periodically, such as a daily tip, a weekly sale, or horoscopes, will encourage return visits.

Compelling Copy

What information does your target audience need to help them make a buying decision? What would you tell a prospective customer that he or she may not know now? If you have no experience writing sales copy, you will want to get some professional help. But you cannot expect a copywriter to understand your business and be able to sell your products without your help. It is up to you to provide the on-target information that is needed.

What information brought your prospect to your website? Use the same concept to create a headline, and your visitors will know that they are in the right place as soon as they sign on. A compelling headline will grab attention and begin the sales process in a powerful way. Supporting copy should follow the same tried-and-true principles used in direct mail. Copy on the Web, however, should have more subheads and shorter sentences.

Two-Way Communication

Autoresponders. A successful website will generate lots of customer inquiries. You could need an assistant to answer your customer's questions instantly; deliver your sales letters, price lists, order forms, and order updates by e-mail; help you develop a mailing list; and work for you twenty-four hours a day, seven days a week. Don't panic. There is a way to automate all of these jobs by using an autoresponder.

Autoresponders, sometimes called autobots, infobots, mailbots, or e-mail-on-demand, are actually simple text files that you put together with information you want your customers to have. Even if you have a power failure and your computer and telephone don't work, your autoresponders will continue working around the clock.

By assigning a specific purpose and a special e-mail address for each one of your autoresponders, you can instantly provide sales information in response to a request from your potential customer. Autoresponders can also help you automate your follow-ups.

Other Communication Tools. Any method that will help you capture your visitor's e-mail address and his or her opinion will help you increase business. A link to your e-mail should be displayed on your main page and repeated on subsequent pages. You can create a guest book and ask your visitors to sign in before gaining complete access to your site. Asking for an opinion and providing questionnaires will aid your market research. One of the most valuable and time-saving features you can put on your website is a FAQ page. Frequently asked questions can help your prospect learn about your business quickly and will save you lots of time.

Commitment

Your website is a never-ending project. It has a life that must evolve to stay current and keep the interest of your visitors. Unlike the contents of your direct-mail pieces, your work will never be finished. A website is like a living thing: You must care for it or it will die of neglect.

Other Considerations

Creating an Online Store

Customers used to hesitate placing credit card orders on the Internet, but that is usually not an issue anymore. Representatives of the Federal Trade Commission have suggested that it is as safe or safer to transmit your credit card number over the Internet than to say it over a cordless telephone or hand it to a waiter in a restaurant.

You will have to decide if you want to accept credit card orders on your website. If so, you will want to offer encryption. Some websites give you the option of phoning in your credit card number and will keep a record of it in their computer. When an order is placed online, the credit card on record is automatically charged. Or you can provide an order form and ask your visitors to print it out and mail it to you with a credit card number or a check. This is not the optimum way to get an order, but it can be adequate when you first start out.

It could be a mistake to set up a fully functioning online store before you establish your website. You may find that your needs are different than first anticipated. Features like shopping carts are not necessary unless you have more than five products to offer.

Affiliate Programs

It is possible to sell products at your website without doing any work at all. Some of the biggest companies on the Internet are willing to form an affiliation with your website that will bring you a percentage of the sales that are elicited from your visitors. For example, if you are selling baby equipment, you can link to the parenting books on Amazon.com and earn between 5 and 15 percent of the sales made. In this case, you can design a bookstore, give your own reviews of the books, and make it as appealing as possible.

The best paying affiliate programs are those for computers, books, travel, music, clothing, toys, flowers, sporting goods, and health products. Consult the appendix for the best resources to help you choose affiliate programs and keep the following points in mind:

- Choose a program that enhances your site and would be of interest to your target audience.
- Only offer products and services that are reputable and reflect your beliefs.

- Make sure you get paid. Some affiliate programs have been known to have problems tracking their orders. Investigate the way this will be done and research their methods.

Website Do's and Don'ts

1. *Do* provide value. When you give your visitors lots of free and useful information and exceptional value, they will learn to love your business and become steady customers.
2. *Do* develop a sense of community. If your website is a meeting place for a group of people who share the same interest, they will be drawn to it. Hosting a chat, forum, or mailing list can help enhance a sense of community.
3. *Do* present your business clearly. A fast-loading, bright, and easy-to-understand site will help your visitors get a quick grasp of what you have to offer and determine that they want to stay a while.
4. *Do* protect your reputation. Tell the truth and don't accept advertising from others who do not. Knowing that they will only encounter information and products that they can trust will go a long way toward building the confidence your visitors need to become customers.
5. *Do* learn about your visitors. Knowing everything you can about your target audience is as important on the Internet as it is in every other area of your business.
6. *Don't* let technology trample marketing. Animated graphics and annoying sounds and music take a long time to load on a computer screen and will distract your visitor from your marketing message.
7. *Don't* create a maze. Your site should be well organized so that visitors can find their way around without getting lost or distracted from your message.
8. *Don't* become static. Add new features on a regular basis and always think of new ways to market your message.
9. *Don't* fail to follow up. The way you handle your customers' inquiries will ultimately determine your level of success. Answer all e-mails promptly and then follow up on a regular basis.
10. *Don't* try to get rich. Having a website will not guarantee that you will become rich. A successful online business cannot be built overnight,

but will grow at a steady pace if you work hard and make the right moves. If making money is your only motive, you won't give enough attention to the details or take the time to create an inviting and informative website.

Promoting Your Website

If you build it, will they come? Yes—but only if you make the right moves. The public needs to know about your website before they can visit. To be successful, you need to market your website using all of the traditional marketing techniques you have learned and then incorporate those that are unique to the Internet. If you combine the best real-world and online promotion techniques, your website will become a well-known Internet destination.

Attracting Traffic

On the Web, traffic is a good thing, and there are no unwelcome visitors. But a large number of hits to your site will not guarantee success. To make the right impact, you must attract members of your target audience, and then give them a reason to come back again.

The energy you put into promoting your website will come back to you in the form of increased traffic. To accomplish the most for your time, concentrate on the following marketing opportunities.

Your Most Important Marketing Tool: E-zines

E-zines (or online newsletters) are extremely effective marketing tools that can help promote your website, garner free publicity, generate advertising revenue for you, and much more. When you offer a free e-zine on your website, visitors will give you their e-mail addresses when they subscribe. This list of e-zine subscribers can become your most valuable asset.

Each time you e-mail one of your e-zines, you have another chance to turn your prospects into customers and remind your existing customers to visit your site. Since this is a true opt-in list, everyone on your list has an interest in your business. Your e-zine gives you the opportunity to send product announcements and updates and promote your website. You must be careful: These subscribers expect lots of free content in your e-zine. If you do not supply interesting articles, you will be inundated with requests to "unsubscribe."

When you publish your own e-zine, you also have the opportunity to trade advertising with the publishers of other e-zines. Even if they do not want to trade, you can find very reasonably priced advertising opportunities in e-zines. Just make sure that you choose a publication that will be of interest to your target market.

At HomeWorkingMom.com, we publish a weekly e-zine titled *HomeWorking Mom-to-Mom Memo*. We have more than 75,000 subscribers, and 1,000 new subscribers sign up each week. Readers write to us with compliments, and the traffic to our website increases after each issue is sent.

Before you can start publishing your e-zine, you have to have a plan. To help you, there are e-zine resources in the appendix. Here are the ten basic steps you must take to start your own e-zine:

1. Develop a theme for your e-zine that will appeal to your target market.
2. Choose a name that will convey its contents.
3. Decide who will write it and explore sources of free content. You may also attract writers who are willing to provide articles in return for links to their e-mail or website.
4. Create a Table of Contents and make a template of standing articles that you can follow each month.
5. Decide the frequency and schedule of your mailings.
6. Determine how the e-zine will be e-mailed.
7. Establish a classified advertising policy.
8. Offer the free e-zine on your website.
9. Write a description of your new e-zine in twenty-five words or less.
10. Send out press releases and announcements about your e-zine.

Search Engines

Everyone has heard of Yahoo! and Google, but there are hundreds more search engines. You can hire a service that will help you register your site, but you want to concentrate on the top search engines and do those registrations yourself. Make sure you include Google, Yahoo!, Bing, Ask.com, and AOL Search. Go to each of these sites and look for the "Add URL" link. On Yahoo!, you must go to the specific page in the directory to submit your URL. Some of these sites are starting to charge for top positions in each category, but you can still get your site listed without paying.

Remember that list of keywords you created when planning your site? Those words will also help you register your website with search engines. You may be asked for keywords or a short description of your site. Make sure that your keywords are actually words that appear on your home page. You can register individual pages of your website on the search engines, increasing the ways in which your target audience can find you.

Social Media

Social media uses technology to enhance social interaction with words. There are many social networking websites, but the three most important ones are Facebook, Twitter, and YouTube.

You may have the impression that these sites are a wasteland for people who are obsessed with putting every move they make online. Those people do exist, but there are real ways that you can promote your website and your mail order business using social media. Immediate communication with your customers and potential customers is possible when you participate in one of these websites. You have the opportunity to personalize your brand and spread the word about your business in a conversational and friendly manor. Each time you add information to your website, you can post a link on Facebook or tweet the link on Twitter.

The good news about social networking is that it works very well. The bad news is that Twitter and Facebook require daily attention. If you are not consistent with your message you will lose all the benefits. YouTube is a little more flexible. To get ideas for how you could put your message on YouTube, search for topics of interest and see what is there now. You can face the camera and demonstrate your product, or you could do a demonstration that does not require a person in the picture. If your YouTube video is entertaining or unusual in any way, it could become a "viral" sensation and attract a large number of viewers.

Write Articles

There are over 1,000 article directories online where you can post an article you've written for free. One of the largest article directories is at www.EzineArticles.com. Other website owners can come to an article directory and put your article on their website as long as they include the resource box that links back to your website or any other link you want to promote.

Articles placed in directories are almost always picked up by search engines like Google. If someone is searching for the topic of your article and clicks on the link they

PROFIT PROFILE: Ruth Townsend, E-zine Queen

Ruth Townsend sat at her desk and asked herself, "Do I really need the stress and frustration of this job?" She had her answer when she grabbed her purse and walked out the door. Ruth felt great. She was free, independent . . . and unemployed. How would she support herself?

With time on her hands and a computer that she barely knew how to turn on, she started surfing the Internet looking for opportunities. She decided that she would sell other people's products online. Realizing that online newsletters—e-zines—were the most targeted place to advertise, she went searching for the right ones.

Researching e-zines was more difficult than she had imagined. First, she had to discover the titles available, and then she wanted to know the content, the circulation, and the cost of advertising in each one. It was a long and tedious process. And then it hit her! Other advertisers must be going through the same trouble. "Right then, I stopped mining for gold on the Net. I decided to go into business selling a tool for other people to use, the same way people got rich selling pickaxes to forty-niners searching for gold in California 150 years ago," Ruth explained. She had found a need and filled it by creating The Directory of Ezines. Her directory was not a printed publication, but a searchable database located at her website, www.lifestylespub.com.

Ruth offered free listings to the publishers, and users could access the online database for a yearly fee of $39.95. The word spread fast; within one day, sixty publishers had asked to sign up. They knew that it would help them attract advertisers and subscribers. After one year in business, her website attracted more than 6,000 visitors each month and her income exceeded her corporate staff job. Users can point and click for information on e-zines sorted in ten different ways, from the name of the e-zine, to the circulation, to the publisher's e-mail address—or a combination of these. A radio interviewer dubbed her "The E-zine Queen," but she did not let that title go to her head. Although her kingdom is the Internet, she said, "I reign from a tiny spare bedroom in my apartment." In 2002, Ruth Townsend retired and sold her directory of Ezines to Charlie Page.

will read your article and may go to your website and purchase your product. You can also promote your articles on Facebook and Twitter.

When submitting an article to an article directory, make sure that the topic of your article is compatible with the subjects covered by that directory.

Don't think you can write an article? Go to: www.WriteEasyArticles.com.

Linking with Other Sites

You will want to have a link page on your site for several reasons. Your visitors will appreciate learning about other sites that cover the same or complementary material and will consider the links part of your free content. Additionally, trading links with other sites can bring increased traffic to your site.

How do you get other sites to link with yours? First, choose websites that are compatible with yours but not necessarily in competition. E-mail the Webmaster of that site and put its URL in the subject line, which will encourage the recipient to open and read the e-mail. Inside, offer to trade reciprocal links and explain why it would be beneficial for the website and its visitors. Follow up at least once if you do not receive a reply.

Traditional Marketing

When promoting your website, don't forget the traditional marketing methods that you've learned so far. Yes, you want to promote online, but marketing in the real world works as well or better. You can bring major traffic to your website if you:

- Send out press releases about your business (include your URL) and specifically about your website. It is easier to get publicity when you have a useful website. If the writer or producer looks at it and likes it, you are in—much easier and more effective than sending a package of information that might not be read.
- Create a small catalog or flyer featuring your best products. Mail it to your customers and potential customers and send them to your website to see more and make purchases.
- Put your website address on everything: business cards, stationery, envelopes, and advertisements. Have color postcards printed with your website logo on the front of the card and a marketing message on the back. Send the cards to everyone on your mailing list.

Common Online Marketing Questions

Q: What can I do so that online prospects won't resent my marketing efforts?

A: Don't send unsolicited e-mail. Instead, participate in online dialogues, always offer free information, and give useful information to attract attention. If you have a website, offer a free e-zine to help start an e-mailing list.

Q: Is there a way to use social media that is easier than posting daily on Twitter and Facebook?

A: Yes. You can also make comments under blogs about your topic or articles that appear online and work your website address into the comment. Keep your comments pertinent and give the reader a reason to want to look at your website.

Q: Is autoresponder e-mail like fax-on-demand?

A: Yes, the principle is the same; however, if your customers are online, autoresponder e-mail is easier for them and less expensive for you. Fax-on-demand often requires a more elaborate setup, and service bureaus can be costly. There are usually two telephone calls involved: the one your customer makes to you, and the one your company makes to return the fax. Autoresponder e-mail can be charged at a monthly flat rate, but toll-free telephone calls to you and sending the responding fax will add to your telephone bill.

08 eBay Your Way To Mail Order Success

There is no doubt that selling online has rejuvenated and expanded the opportunities available to mail order business owners, because Internet auctions are one of the easiest and least expensive ways to sell your products. Auction websites like eBay have made it possible for home-based businesses to compete with the big guys. On eBay, you can sell your mail order products and establish a successful online presence with or without your own website. According to eBay's corporate website, there are more than 90 million eBay users worldwide who trade $1,900 worth of goods every second of the day. If you are willing to learn the right moves, some of that cash can go into your pocket.

Why You Should Sell on eBay

Why wouldn't you sell on eBay? If you own a mail order business, you want as many chances to attract customers as possible. No matter what else you do, why would you ignore a chance to put your products before millions of customers? Fees on eBay are low when you compare them to the cost of doing a direct mail promotion or buying advertising. Your selling opportunities are worldwide if you choose to sell your goods internationally. All of the international eBay websites can be accessed at the bottom of the main page.

An eBay auction is a great way to test your mail order product idea. If there is enough interest to generate sales on eBay, it is likely that you will be able to sell your products using the other mail order methods. Testing on eBay can be a way to save a lot of upfront money. Keep in mind that most eBay shoppers are looking for the best price available whether it is an auction or "Buy It Now" product. It is common for those wanting to buy an item they see on other websites to go to eBay first to compare prices. When you discover a product that is in high demand that you can promote effectively and sell for a low price, eBay success—and home-based mail order success—will be yours.

What You Should Sell on eBay

Getting started on eBay is as simple as registering and following the easy steps. But first, you need a product to sell. Finding a product source that is affordable, repeatable, and unlimited is your ultimate goal. But in the beginning, you will probably have to be a lot more creative. For example, there are foods available only in the U.S. that are desired by people in Europe. Some examples of these are: Lucky Charms cereal (popular in the U.K. and Ireland because of the leprechaun), certain cookies, candies, and powdered drink mixes. Americans buy these items in their local Walmart and put them on eBay. As you can see from this example, when you are selling on eBay, research is key.

Not only do you need to find products that will sell on eBay, you need to find a way to get them at a price that allows a significant profit. If you have a home-based mail order business, you should test out your products and expand your options by selling those items on eBay. If you don't have a product line yet and you think that eBay may be a good way to start your business, you have a world of possibilities when choosing a product. You also have a lot of research and trial and error ahead of you. If you are persistent, you will discover products you can source that will sell. If you give up after your first failure, you will never have that eBay business you dream about.

If you have a good idea of what you want to sell, you can do your research right on eBay. After you sign into your account, you will be able to see how previous auctions have ended. Click on "Advanced Search" and enter the category of product you are looking for. Then, choose "Completed Listings" before you actually start the search. Listings in red did not sell. Green listings show what was recently sold in that category. Make notes about the name brands and go back and search each brand for more information. Once you know the total number of completed auctions for an item, you can divide the number of "solds" by the total number of listings to find out the sale percentage for that item. This type of research should be an ongoing project so that you can spot changes in the trends.

If you don't know what you want to sell and need information about the bestselling items on eBay, you can pay for an expensive program or you can find out what's hot in almost every category for free. Go to www.pulse.ebay.com. You will see the top ten searches on eBay right now and you can also search each of the sub-categories.

One final note: eBay trends can be influenced by what is happening in the world. Stay informed about current events and, if you can act quickly, you can turn an event into a product that will give you short-term success.

Where To Find Products

There are a variety of product resources available to you. If you use creative thinking and communicate with other eBay sellers, you will be able to discover even more places to get your products at a good price. Each has its positive and negative aspects. Here are just some of the options you can consider:

1. *Wholesale and Drop-shipping.* The most important thing you need to know about both these options is this: Be careful. There are a lot of misleading offers and plain and simple scams out there that you should avoid. In both cases, you want to deal directly with the manufacturer and avoid the middlemen. If a company is seeking your business it is probably not in your best interest to buy from them. In order for a manufacturer to seriously consider selling to you, you need to have three things: 1. You need to have filed a DBA (doing business as) certificate with your county government. 2. You have to have a tax ID that authorizes you to collect sales tax. (Don't worry about collecting taxes unless you are selling new merchandise to someone who lives in the same state as you do.) 3. You need a business checking account.
2. *Garage sales and estate sales.* Although garage sales can be a good source of merchandise at a great price, you have to weed through a lot of junk in order to find something you can resell. On the other hand, estate sales contain everything from a household and the possibility of finding valuable items is increased. Know what you are looking for before you attend a sale, and when you make an offer have the money in your hand. It is hard to reject an offer when all the seller has to do is reach out and claim the cash. You can get a lot of bargains that way.
3. *Buy on eBay.* There are many eBay sellers who are lazy or have not taken the time to inform themselves on the best ways to sell. They may have good merchandise at a good price, but if no one sees their auction, it won't be successful. You can find these ignored auctions and buy a product at a very low price. It will then be your job to start a new auction using your best techniques. You can also search for "wholesale lots" on eBay. If you buy in bulk you can save money and resell the items individually.

4. *Buy retail.* If you have a Walmart or any of the dollar store chains in your community, you have a resource that others may not have. Thrift stores are also a place to peruse on a regular basis to look for vintage items. After doing your research on eBay, go shopping! A product that you pay $1 for could sell for $5 or more, which is a 400 percent profit! If you begin to specialize in one niche, such as baby clothes or cosmetics, you will know exactly what to look for on your shopping trips and your potential customers will get the impression that you have a special resource.
5. *Have it made.* People feel strongly about their sports teams and their politics. You could come up with a good slogan and have T-shirts made. I know a young Yankees baseball fan who made some cash on eBay by making T-shirts. It was 2003, and the Boston Red Sox had not won the World Series since 1918. As the two teams faced each other in game 7 of the American League Series, Yankees third baseman Aaron Boone hit a home run to clinch their entry into the World Series. This young fan had T-shirts made to taunt Red Sox fans and laud the Yankees past and present that had insured their failure. He called the Yankee players the "Killer B's"—Babe, Boone, Bucky, and Buckner. The T-shirts cost $5 each to be made. One T-shirt sold at auction for more than $60! The others sold for approximately $20 each.
6. *Share information.* There is a place on eBay for sellers to communicate. Just click on the Community tab and you will see a drop-down box that will give you choices for Groups and Discussions. You can find information about hot-selling products and how to access them. There are also Facebook groups on a variety of eBay topics that you can join for free. You don't have to do this alone.
7. *Get it for free.* There are a lot of people who hate clutter and give away unwanted items for free. In fact, many put perfectly good items out with the trash. Drive around a neighborhood with expensive houses after the trash has been put out, and you might find lots of items you can sell with little or no repair. If you like to refinish furniture, this could be a wonderful way to find items. Put the word out to friends and family that you want their unwanted items. You can even offer to share the profits with them. You could also locate free stuff on at www.Craigslist.com. There is a section for listing free items. If you find something you think you can sell, your only cost will be getting the item in your hands.

Promoting Your Listings

Selling on eBay is extremely competitive. Those who take the time to promote their listings get more traffic to their listings. More traffic means more sales. Once a potential buyer comes to your auction, your photos and the way your product is listed have to keep them there. Keep the following points in mind to get the maximum number of clicks on your listing:

- Your product photo image should show on the preview that buyers see in their search results. The photo will allow your listing to stand out and you can put a short sales message such as "free shipping" at the bottom of the image.
- Your headline is much more than a title. It must contain the search terms that buyers will use so that your listing comes up in their searches. Then, you need to separate your listing from the crowd by including a unique selling position, such as "free shipping," "lowest price on eBay," or "free gift included."
- There are free ways to make your title stand out. For example, you can use upper case letters at the beginning of each word or include some allowed symbols. If your potential profit can cover the cost, enhance your listing with bold letters and a subtitle that encourages the buyer to act now.
- Write a creative but accurate product description. You can answer the questions that you get asked most within the description to avoid buyer inquiries. More than facts and figures are required. The buyer wants to know how this product will benefit his life and it is your job to create a listing that will help him visualize those benefits. If your listing is long, be sure to repeat your call to action at least three times. If you are offering free shipping, your buyer needs to know that. Don't forget—a listing that looks good will attract more customers.
- End your auctions on Sunday night—the time when there is a lot of traffic on eBay.
- The feedback your customers give you is vitally important on eBay. Most buyers check your feedback before buying from you. Ask for feedback after a sale and offer to return the favor. Making customer service a priority will help assure that all your feedback will be good.

- Participate in the eBay community. You can start an eBay blog (find the option under Community) and write about your product or anything else that will increase your appeal to buyers or other sellers.

Increase Your Profits with Great Photos

A picture is worth a thousand words and could be worth a lot of dollars on eBay. A bad auction photo will cost you sales. People want to see what they are buying and your photo is the only way that can happen. It is possible to take great photos for your eBay listings with a digital camera. You don't need an expensive camera to take great photos. The first photo on your listing is free. You can pay to add additional photos or upload your photos on a free photo hosting website and give the buyers a link. With a little preparation, your photos can look professional and answer all the questions your potential buyers might have.

First, prepare your product. Make sure it is dust-free and in the best condition possible. Put a plain white backdrop so that nothing distracts from the item. You can use a piece of poster board, but make sure the dull side is towards the camera. If the item is white, use another neutral color. If your item is larger, use a white sheet as background. Now it is time to choose your lighting. If you can take your photo outside on an overcast day, that is the best light you can use. If this is not possible, take your photo by a window. If you are taking your photo at night, you can use lamp lighting but take off the lampshade.

Take a lot of photos; you can always delete the ones you don't like. Get close-ups of all the important parts and fill the frame of the photo as much as possible. If size is important, put a coin in the photo or a ruler to give perspective. Take photos from different angles. Choose the main photo and then the detailed shots as needed. For example, if you are selling china, take a close-up of the information on the back of the plate.

Order Fulfillment/Feedback

To accept payments on eBay, the majority of sellers use eBay-owned PayPal.

Even before you sell your first item, you should have your shipping supplies and know what costs will be involved.

You will need tape, tape dispensers, scissors, labels, and a scale. The USPS offers free priority mail supplies that include mailing containers of various sizes, labels, and

PROFIT PROFILE: Steve Weber, eBay Expert

Steve Weber did not know that putting some old books up for auction would change his life. He really didn't know what to expect. But when the twelve books sold quickly, he couldn't wait to find more books to list. He took $80 out of his savings account and bought four bags of used paperback books from a local shop. Some didn't sell, but one sold for $23, and by the time he sold half of the books he had doubled his $80 investment. He was hooked.

Next came a carload of books bought at a library sale, and two months later he had quit his job to sell used books on eBay full-time. He eventually expanded to other auction sites and other types of auctions and today he has done $1.4 million in sales to 130,000 customers in all fifty states and thirty-one countries. "Having freedom from a nine-to-five job is a great feeling, very empowering," he told me. "Knowing that you can rely on yourself for your income instead of a boss gives you a lot of security."

Steve believes in helping others achieve success on eBay because he feels that everyone can win. "The more people who become buyers and sellers in this worldwide network, the more valuable it is for everyone to belong," he says. In fact, asking for advice is what Steve recommends to all aspiring eBay sellers. "Don't be afraid to ask for advice, and learn from the mistakes of others." Because of his desire to help others, Steve now writes books to help others duplicate his success. He tells all his eBay secrets in his book, *eBay 101: Selling on eBay For Part-time or Full-time Income. Beginner to Power Seller in 90 Days* (Weber books). His other books are listed in the appendix.

Steve uses eBay to sell collectibles, but feels that Amazon.com is a better place to sell media items like books, CDs, and DVDs. He advises that those who want to sell handmade or vintage items go to www.Etsy.com.

When asked what are the biggest mistake new sellers make and what power sellers do that others don't, his answer was the same: Concentrate on customer service. "New sellers have trouble giving customers the benefit of the doubt," he explains. "If a customer claims that they haven't received their package or that they need to return an item, meet them halfway, even if you are not required to do so." He believes customer service is a key ingredient to a power seller's success too. "Take care of details and prevent customer service issues instead of reacting to problems."

tape. They offer flat-rate shipping that could cost more but simplifies the process. A small flat-rate box ships up to three pounds for $4.95.

The faster you fill your orders and answer buyer inquiries, the more money you will make on eBay because the feedback you receive from buyers will determine your long-term success. You can be rated positive, neutral, or negative. Buyers and sellers will be able to leave up to eighty characters describing how much they liked or disliked their experience buying from you.

You will also be rated on a scale from one to five stars based on the following questions:

1. How accurate was the item description?
2. How satisfied were you with the seller's communication?
3. How quickly did the seller ship the item?
4. How reasonable were the shipping and handling charges?

Dissatisfied customers will be sure to give you a bad rating. If you have done a good job fulfilling the order, ask the customer to give you a good rating and always return the favor.

Common eBay Questions

Q: I want to make a lot of money on eBay. What should I do first? Should I try to find a good product to sell or find a good source for products?

A: You may have heard the eternal question, "What came first . . .the chicken or the egg?" On eBay, the eternal question is, "What comes first . . . the product you will sell or the product source?" Do you search your sources until you find an appealing product? Or, do you determine your product and then find a good source? You can be successful either way, but you increase your chances if you choose a proven product first.

Q: How do I decide if I should list my product as an auction or a "Buy It Now?"

A: When you do your research on eBay, your search results will show the auctions and the Buy It Now listings together. To get an accurate answer, separate them into two separate categories. You can choose "just auctions" or "just Buy It Now." That will help you determine which method was more successful for that particular product.

09 No-Mail Mail Order

The Most Profitable Online Business Is . . . Information! People have always been willing to pay for information. Just visit a bookstore on a Saturday afternoon and analyze your fellow customers as they look for information on health-related issues, career or business start-ups, gardening, investing—you name a topic and you can be sure that a book has been written about it. In the past, when faced with a new challenge, interest, or event in our lives, there were only two ways to get the information we needed: We could consult an expert or consult a book. Today, the Internet is often the first tool used to seek out information, and savvy mail order entrepreneurs are making millions as information providers.

Digital Delivery = No-Mail Mail Order

When shopping online first became popular and profitable, many people joked that it was very convenient to order online, but it was too bad that the product could not be delivered right through the computer. How great would it be if you could purchase a pair of shoes, a camera, or a piece of jewelry and download your purchase for immediate use?

This concept is actually possible today. No, you can't transmit a diamond bracelet through your computer, but you can instantly deliver information online.

Selling information online presents many advantages for mail order businesses. Digital delivery eliminates the need for expensive printed materials, envelopes, and postage. There is no need for order processing or mail handling. Unlike traditional mail order businesses, you can work in a tiny space when you are selling information online because no product storage is necessary.

Besides the cost-saving factor, the best reason to sell information products online is the immediate response you can give and receive. Your information can be delivered instantly to your customer, and your payment is made on the spot. This gives your customer instant gratification, and you gain the ability to analyze and predict the response you receive and adjust your marketing efforts to maximize your profits.

Determining the Best Information to Sell

You may be wondering what in the world you know or can find out that people would be willing to pay for. Believe it or not, you have expertise in many areas and the ability to access information and package it in a marketable format.

If you begin to feel frustrated as you work on determining the type of information you would like to sell, keep one thing in mind: Information is a no-limit business that may require some up-front work, but you only have to produce it once. You won't run out of stock or have to purchase any raw materials. There will be very little work required after you complete your creation, and you can sell it forever.

Traditionally, writers are advised to write about what they know. This is also good advice for those looking for information to sell online, but don't limit your options. You can also pick a topic, any topic at all that interests you, and do enough research to become a self-proclaimed expert. If you are interested, chances are a significant number of other people will be too.

Here's a good example: Leo Quinn teaches a very popular class on how to get out of debt. He decided to put the information from the class into e-book form. Now he can bring his message to an unlimited number of people and has created an additional profit stream.

Write down a preliminary list of topics you might like to cover, and do some research. Discuss your list with friends and family and see if they express interest. Search the Internet for information sources to see if enough raw material is there that will help you create your product. Don't be discouraged if you find that others have already produced a similar product. You can always introduce a new and better version.

Tips for Writing Your Information Product

1. Write down the exact focus of your information product. What problem are you trying to solve? What need are you trying to fill?

2. Write down at least ten questions about your topic. What would the reader want to know?
3. Transform your questions into subheadlines, forming a kind of outline for your product.
4. Under each subheadline, write up to ten more questions.
5. Answer each of the questions. Try to fill at least one page with each answer.
6. If you are an inexperienced writer, remember to write as you speak. Don't be formal or use big words to make an impression. Your reader will appreciate a one-to-one tone much more. If you have trouble, try recording your information and then transcribing your responses.
7. Don't try to be perfect. If you edit your information as you write, it will slow you down. Get the information written and then wait at least one day before you go back and edit your material.
8. Send your finished product for free to websites on your topic and ask for a review that you can reprint. Make corrections based on any negative feedback you receive.
9. Remember: Because you do not have to have your product printed, you can change and improve your digital product as time goes on.

Selling What You Know

How-to Instructions

If you can solve a problem, you can get sales—lots of them. Your target audience has many problems. You just have to determine what they are and come up with solutions that you've discovered in your own life or by doing research. Did you devise a quick way to get your toddler to toilet train? That method could become an e-book that would be of interest to many parents. Are your vegetable and flower gardens flourishing? Write about your techniques and sell your expertise. If you are in one of the helping professions like nursing, coaching, nutrition, or finance, you can be paid for online consultations by e-mail or develop an online newsletter and charge a fee.

Business Ideas and Advice

There are a lot of people making a lot of money offering business ideas and advice on the Internet. In fact, this is one of the top categories of information products. Just

PROFIT PROFILE: Rita Woods, HomeJobStop.com

Rita Woods wanted to work at home so that she could spend more time with her young daughter. She searched for legitimate Internet opportunities but did not feel comfortable with any home job site. Rita decided to do her own research about the home job market and create a home job site that could be trusted to be 100 percent truthful. In other words, Rita Woods found a need and filled it by creating a very special online information product.

"My first step in creating HomeJobStop.com was research," Rita recalls. "I read the stories of other stay-at-home moms and dads and entered chats and various message boards online asking job seekers to share their needs." Rita then developed a loose plan for researching the home job market. "When I encountered a problem I couldn't fix, I just changed my approach," she says.

Although she had a fear of failure and was facing financial hardship during the months that she was creating her site, Rita did not give up her dream. "During the months that I spent creating the site, our finances dwindled to nothing. In December of 2000, just before our launch, I sold the only piece of jewelry I owned: one ring. I got $90 for it," Rita relates. On December 21, 2000, Rita sold her first membership to HomeJobStop.com and has never looked back.

Every home job on HomeJobStop.com is carefully evaluated, categorized, and verified before it appears before the members. "If I have any doubt, I apply to the job myself to see what happens," Rita explains. Every step of the way, Rita has kept focused on her mission to create a reliable home job resource. "We do the guesswork so that our members don't go 'emotionally broke' trying to discern good opportunities from poor opportunities."

HomeJobStop.com has a combination of local and national opportunities in its database, which is updated daily. For a low, one-time fee members are given lifetime access to the site. "Lifetime access allows us the opportunity to establish a long-lasting relationship with our members, which makes it all worthwhile," Rita says.

about everyone wants to make more money, and many people would like to start their own business.

James Jones is one of the information entrepreneurs who has perfected his research methods enough to create more than one membership website. In what is really an e-book that can be read online with password access or downloaded, James created *Secret Underground Business Plans, Projects and Ideas* after eighteen months of research. He compiled more than 400 pages of little-known, home-based businesses people are running from their homes that can be copied. For example, he describes how a woman in Georgia provides a high-demand service to parents that takes about sixty minutes of her time yet nets her an average of $120 per job.

Lists

Researching a topic and then compiling a list can be one of the easiest information products to start, but it will probably require more updating than other types of information. There are websites that list home-based job information (see Profit Profile: Rita Woods, HomeJobStop.com). Other list sites offer topics such as opportunities for freelance writers and houses in foreclosure.

Packaging Your Information for Sale

e-Books

When is a book not really a book? When it is an e-book (electronic book). We live in a society that wants information without delay. That's why e-books are the perfect online information product. They can be available for instant downloading after payment. Although e-books are shown online with "covers," this is just a marketing technique. Resources you can use to create an e-book on your favorite topic are included in the appendix.

Sometimes an e-book is given away for free as a marketing tool. If you offer a free e-book on your website, it can attract more visitors. When you develop an e-book and give it away for free, you will not only be providing your target audience with some valuable, free information, you will also be able to incorporate information about your products and services, and increase your sales. At my website www.HomeworkingMom.com, we offer a free e-book titled *Work-At-Home Job Finder For Moms*. I invite you to take a look.

PROFIT PROFILE: MyMoneyandShopping.com

In chapter 7 we met Angela Smith, who has deep knowledge of the Internet and helps others make money online. As many entrepreneurs do, Angela has always worked at a variety of part-time jobs to earn money when she was not earning enough from her Internet business projects. She discovered "secret shopping" and realized that not only was this a great way to earn extra money, it was something that other people might want to learn how to do. To teach others how to get started and succeed in secret shopping, she started a membership website called MyMoneyandShopping.com.

Secret shoppers are paid to visit specific stores and businesses to observe and secretly evaluate the quality of a company's products and customer service. Previous experience is not required. Almost anyone can be a secret shopper. You need to be honest and dependable; be able to read, speak, and write the English language, and have the ability to visit various store locations. How much you make depends on the number and types of shops you agree to do.

Angela has personally earned as much as $840 in two days as a secret shopper, but most shoppers are paid an hourly wage of $10 to $40 per hour and are usually reimbursed for any purchases they are required to make. Payment may take the form of a cash payment for completed assignments, reimbursement for out-of-pocket dollars spent, or a combination of the two. Each assignment has a specific set of guidelines and deadlines. An assignment could be evaluating a restaurant, shopping for an apartment or new car, purchasing linens at a department store, or inquiring about opening a bank account—to name just a few.

"I've worked as a secret shopper for five years and know that it is possible to earn a very good living," Angela explains. "I started MyMoneyandShopping.com in June of 2002, and have enjoyed helping other people earn money, free dinners, hotel stays, merchandise, movies, and more. What other job can improve your lifestyle and put money in your pocket?"

MyMoneyandShopping.com is an excellent example of an information product that has found a way to be bigger and better than the competition. There are a lot of sites offering to help aspiring secret shoppers, but MyMoneyandShopping.

com is different, mostly because Angela sees the big picture and meets the needs of both the secret shoppers and the job schedulers. Angela gives lots of personal attention to her members and even sends out e-mails directly to members when she learns of new secret shopping opportunities in their geographical area. "The best part about our fast growth is that many secret shopping companies want to work with us. This has enabled us to bring some exclusive and first-look shops to our members so they are in the right place at the right time to get the most desirable assignments," Angela reports. Because job schedulers have a good opinion of MyMoneyandShopping.com's trained shoppers, many are willing to give MyMoneyandShopping.com's members the first chance to learn about new secret shopping assignments when they become available.

MyMoneyandShopping.com is also an excellent example of an information product that uses the paid membership model as a way to package the concept. The site has thousands of members and has been very successful. Because Angela uses ClickBank (see appendix) to process her sales, she has also been able to develop her own affiliate program. Other websites highly recommend MyMoneyandShopping.com and if they make a sale they receive a 50 percent commission. ClickBank takes care of paying the affiliates automatically so there is no extra work involved.

Membership or Paid Access Websites

Internet users are getting used to the idea that some websites charge for access when they contain information that is not freely available. There are many examples of membership websites. The Profit Profiles in this chapter illustrate two. Both HomeJobStop.com and MoneyandShopping.com are continually updated. Home JobStop.com charges a one-time fee for lifetime access. MyMoneyandShopping .com charges a yearly rate but also has a lifetime option that includes access to its sister site, MoneyandSurveys.com, for a higher fee. Other membership sites charge a monthly access fee.

Paid Online Newsletter Subscriptions

Because there are so many free newsletters offered online, it is difficult to get paid subscribers for an online newsletter. Some successful paid subscriptions convert free subscribers to paid subscribers by mentioning content that is available in the paid or pro version of their newsletter. Other newsletters offer free trials or a free gift to drive subscriptions. In all cases, the content of a paid newsletter must be superior.

Pricing Your Information Product

Information products can range from $5 special reports to high-end, detailed financial newsletters costing $400 to $500 a year. The price of an information product depends on how exclusive and how accessible the information is, how much ongoing support you will provide, and the expenses involved. When selling information online, you can ask for a one-time fee or a monthly access charge.

You will probably invest a significant amount of time while researching and writing your information product, but the amount of money you need to get started is minimal. If your idea doesn't work, your biggest investment has been time, and the time you spend trying out a business idea is never wasted when you learn from your mistakes and keep moving toward your goal.

The best way to price your information product is to find others in your category and determine the going rate. If you are selling an information product that needs constant updating, you might consider charging more than if you just do the work once and keep selling the same information over and over again.

Managing the Sale and Digital Delivery

You no longer have to have your own merchant account in order to accept payment over the Internet. There are services that will accept your customers' credit card or electronic check payment for you and then notify you when the transaction has been completed. PayPal is one of the most popular choices. Other payment processing companies are listed in the appendix.

PayPal

PayPal enables any business or individual with an e-mail address to accept or make a payment online. It can be used to sell both online information products and any other mail order products that will be sent through the mail.

There are no set-up fees, and the per-transaction fees are low. Your customers do not need to join PayPal in order to make a payment. They just supply their credit card information as they would with any other purchase on PayPal's secure server. When a purchase is made, PayPal notifies you by e-mail and tells you how much was paid and gives you the customer's information. You can then notify the buyer where to go to download his or her purchase, or package the item and mail it.

To get more information, go to www.paypal.com.

Common Online Information Product Questions

Q: What is the best way to do research for an online information product I'd like to develop?

A: Researching an information product can be easily accomplished without leaving your desk chair when you use the resources available to you online. First, check an online bookstore such as Amazon.com to see what books they have on your topic. This will give you a chance to place an online order for the best books while you are doing your online research. Then, type your topics into search engines like Google and Yahoo. You will discover websites, e-books, and other unexpected sources of information. Then, visit message boards and discussion groups on your topic. Message boards are listed at www.ezboard.com and www.delphi.com/delphi. You can find all sorts of discussion lists at www.topica.com and www.yahoogroups.com.

Q: How can I quickly test an idea for an online information product?

A: The fastest way to test interest in a topic is to use pay-per-click search engines such as Overture and Google Adwords (www.adwords.google.com). For each of these methods, you pay only when an interested person clicks on your link. Pay-per-click search engines and ads also provide information on the number of clicks each of your keywords has received in the past month. If you have not developed your online information product yet, you can try an affiliate program on the same or related topic and send the "click" to the affiliate website. This is also a way to promote affiliate programs without owning your own website.

10 The Mail Room

Your mail room may not be big—or even a room. But the systems you develop for processing mail and fulfilling orders will be at the heart of your home-based mail order business. It is important to establish procedures for incoming and outgoing mail as quickly as possible. Fast, friendly service is the ultimate key to success in mail order. The most detailed business plan or marketing concept will be rendered useless unless you can handle your orders and inquiries without delay. Even if you are getting only one or two orders per day right now, you need to be ready for the day when you go to get your mail and the mailbox is overflowing with orders and inquiries.

Mail is only one of the ways that your business will receive inquiries and orders. Inquiries received by telephone can be handled using the system detailed in this chapter. Online inquiries can be handled economically with an autoresponder e-mail address (see chapter 7). To accept telephone or computer-generated orders, however, you must have the ability to accept credit cards. As we discussed in chapter 3, it has always been difficult for home-based businesses to obtain credit card merchant accounts through banks, which is the way that Visa and MasterCard operate. American Express and Discover Card are two companies that do not use banks as intermediaries, making them less difficult to deal with; however, the large number of home-based businesses being started has attracted the attention of independent service organizations that will grant home businesses merchant status. Compare rates, equipment costs, and application fees. The Profit Profile of Merchant Warehouse in this chapter details one good option.

There are general goals you should have when designing a successful mail-management program. To be successful you will want to consider the following:

- *Process orders fast.* If possible, all orders should be shipped within twenty-four hours. If payment is made by check, ship as soon as the check clears.
- *Acknowledge back orders immediately.* If the order cannot be shipped immediately, your customer should know why.
- *Always include a bounce-back offer in every outgoing package.* It is good customer service to let your customers know about related products or services or to give them a special offer because they placed an order. A happy customer who just received his or her order may be ready to order again.
- *Answer any inquiries immediately.* The speed with which your potential customers receive their catalogs and other requested materials will influence their perception of your company.
- *Resolve complaints without delay.* It is possible to keep your customer if problems are easily handled.
- *Stand by your guarantee.* If you offer a money-back guarantee, send refunds immediately upon request.

These general goals will be the basis of all the systems you design for your incoming and outgoing mail. Specific procedures to help you save time and money follow.

Managing Incoming Mail

If yours is a solo business, you will have to put aside a few hours each day to process your mail, ship orders, and answer inquiries. You will be receiving two basic kinds of mail: letters containing money (orders) and letters without money. It is important to make this initial separation and then proceed with the mail processing. Of the letters without money, you will have inquiries, customer service problems, and other requests.

You should have a designated location for processing mail. A large table is necessary, along with bins marked for each type of mail you receive. As you open and identify the mail, place the entire letter in the proper processing bin. After you open a letter, staple the envelope on the back to save for reference. When you are finished sorting, you will have piles of inquiries, orders, and customer service questions.

When processing orders paid by check, it is important to keep the check with the order throughout the process. If you separate the check from the order and deposit it immediately, you may realize later that you have an incomplete name and address or are unsure of the check amount. This may seem like basic information, but it is an easy mistake to make.

Once your mail is opened, it is time to process it. Using your computer, your task will be completed quickly.

Why You Need a Computer

At the beginning of this book, I told you that you could start a mail order business without a computer. I stand by that statement, because successful home-based mail order businesses have been run for years using alphabetized index cards and typed mailing lists that were photocopied onto labels. But if you can afford a computer and are willing to develop the basic skills necessary to do data processing, that is the best way to go. Computerizing your home-based mail order business will give you advantages that you will not have access to using index cards. For example, a computer will offer you the following abilities:

- You will only have to type a name and address once. If you handle your orders and inquiries using a typewriter, you will have to type multiple labels: one for your index card, one each time you want to contact the customer, and one to mail each order.
- You will have more flexibility for storing information. Every detail of a customer's order will be on your computer. Much of the information can be coded and easy to record.
- You will have more flexibility for retrieving information. With a computer you can call up a list of all customers living in California whose last names start with M and who ordered in the last 30 days. Or you could instantly locate customers who have made purchases of more than $50. To obtain that kind of information from cards could take hours or days.
- You will be able to analyze sales and other data. By pressing a few buttons you can instantly determine how many orders were received in response to a promotion or on one particular day.
- You can maintain your house list in a format that can be easily corrected and used for your own mailings or to rent to other companies.
- You can prepare form letters for recurring needs and personalize them so it appears that the entire letter was written to an individual customer.

Mail Processing with a Computer

If you are computerizing your orders and inquiries, it is best to finish processing your mail at the computer. There are specialized computer programs designed to help you run your mail order business. I will discuss them later in this chapter. These programs are quite expensive, however, and you may not need them during your start-up phase. As your business becomes more successful, you will need more sophisticated ways to process your mail. For now I will give you an overview of basic procedures.

You should have a mailing program that will allow you to enter the complete name, address, and telephone number of the person placing the order. Before entering the data, check your records to see if this is a repeat customer. Because you could have more than one customer with the same name, you should be able to call up a file by telephone number or other code in addition to name. If there is no existing customer record, a new record needs to be started. Your customer records also need to detail the following points for each order:

- *Item(s) ordered.* You need this information for purposes of fulfillment and inventory.
- *Date of order.* The date defines when the order was received and allows you to choose your most recent customers. It also acts as reference for fulfillment.
- *Amount paid.* Which of your customers spend the most money?
- *Method of payment.* If there is a problem, you need to know the method of payment. You don't want to issue a cash refund if the order was paid by credit card.
- *Sales tax.* You will be required to collect sales tax from customers located within your state. Although this may be changed, right now you are not required to collect sales tax from customers residing in other states. You need a record of the sales tax collected so you will know how much to pay.
- *Key code or source of order.* As we discussed previously, it is important to know the source of your orders so that you can determine what works.

Once you have entered all of the information on your computer, you can separate your checks and prepare them for deposit.

Print out mailing labels that are coded with the items ordered so that the person filling the orders can glance at the label and know what needs to be shipped, or if you are using a mail order program, print out a packing list. If you are unable to do this, you should fill out the packing list by hand on a preprinted form.

Mail Processing without a Computer

If you are operating without a computer, you will need to have a file card system that will help you keep track of your customers and inquirers. One set of cards will contain the names of the people who have requested information. The card should contain all of the information that you would put on a computer record, even though you will not be able to automatically sort the names or generate reports. You want the information to be there for future reference or when you do computerize your business.

Sort your incoming orders into two piles. The first pile will contain orders that came from ads or unsolicited mailings. A new card should be made for these orders. The second pile will contain orders that resulted from a previous inquiry. With an inquiry conversion, the card should be moved from the inquirer file to the customer file. All new orders or customer contacts should be noted on the card.

It can be difficult to type directly on index cards, so it is easier to type a label and paste it on the card. You can either type two labels (one for the card, one for the order) or type a sheet of labels and photocopy it onto another sheet of labels to use for shipping. Cards can be filed by zip code so that your names are in zip code order if you want to type labels for a mailing. A control file of duplicate cards in alphabetical order will help you find customers who have moved.

It is possible to function without a computer. Major catalog companies did so before computers were available. However, you will save time and make more money when you computerize your order processing and mailing lists.

Managing Outgoing Mail

When you use first-class mail, your mail promotions are more likely to be opened. Recipients will subconsciously think that if you spent $.44 or more to mail to them, your message must have worth. If you use stamps instead of putting your postage on with a machine, that will attract more attention and your message is even more likely to be read. There are ways that you can use first-class mail and get some discounts. If you bar code your addresses and presort you can save some money.

While the benefits of first-class mail are real, it becomes impractical and too expensive to mail to your prospects using first-class mail when you promote to

PROFIT PROFILE: Merchant Warehouse

How can you run a home-based mail order business if you cannot accept credit cards? You can't. But some banks refuse to give merchant status to home business owners, making accepting credit cards a difficult, expensive, and sometimes impossible process. If you sell online, there is no problem. You can use PayPal to accept payments from all of the major credit cards. But if you run a mail order business and/or take credit card orders over the telephone, you need a different solution: A MOTO (Mail Order Telephone Order) account.

Merchant Warehouse was founded in 1998 on the principle that businesses should be able to purchase credit card machines and merchant accounts at a reasonable price backed by great customer service. They have recently received the Electronic Transaction Association's ISO of the year award.

Merchant Warehouse specializes in merchant accounts and guarantees the lowest cost of credit card machines, credit card processing, and merchant accounts. To be approved for a merchant account, you need to have a business based in the United States, a business tax ID number, and a U.S. bank account. With a 99 percent approval rate and an average approval time of twenty-four hours, Merchant Warehouse also does not charge a start-up fee or a cancellation fee and all of their contracts are on a month-to-month basis.

To be approved to accept credits cards quickly call Merchant Warehouse now: (866) 761-5531. Or you can go to their website. A special section has been set up for those who respond from this book. You will be able to set-up a merchant account with no application fees, no set-up fees, and no contracts or cancellation/termination fees if you use this link: www.MerchantWarehouse.com/mailorderbusiness.

thousands of people on a regular basis. That is why most mailers that are mailing identical pieces of mail to at least 200 addresses use bulk-rate mail.

Preparing a bulk-rate mailing can be confusing and time-consuming at first, but once you get the knack of it you will appreciate the savings. There are professional mailing companies that will prepare your bulk-rate mailing for you, but the added cost of paying the mailer may be too much for a fledgling mail order business. Even if you do eventually use a mailing company, it will add to your business expertise if you have first-hand experience preparing a bulk mailing.

Consider the following points before you decide to become a bulk-rate mailer:

- Bulk-rate mail will take more time to reach the recipient, especially if it is sent across the country, so be sure to allow a few weeks.
- There is a yearly fee to purchase a bulk-rate permit.
- Your bulk-rate permit number must show on each piece of mail, so consider having it printed on your envelopes, self-mailer brochures, or postcards. Otherwise, you will have to use a rubber stamp or postage meter, which would be very time-consuming.

Mail Handling 101

Whether you are filling orders, answering information requests, or doing direct-mail promotions, your procedures for handling your mail will affect the amount of time and money you spend.

At first you may have only a few orders to fill and letters to answer. But if you make the right moves, you could be dealing with large numbers. Preparing 5,000 letters for a direct mailing or opening up bins of mail received in response to some great publicity can seriously cut into your workday. There is one tip that you should remember when you handle mail: The same job, done repeatedly, will save time. When you try to handle a series of different jobs all at one time, it takes longer to complete the project. For example, one business owner might open a request for information, type a label, stuff, and seal the envelope, put the label and the stamp on the outside of the envelope, seal it, and then go on to the next information request. Done that way, it will take you all day to process the mail.

Instead, when opening a large number of envelopes, slit all of the envelopes open at one time, then go back and separate the contents. When stuffing the envelopes, prepare all of the inserts in advance. Everything should be folded and lined up on the table. Gather one piece from each pile and then insert the entire contents into the envelope at once. Stuff all of the envelopes and then go back and seal them. Put labels on all the envelopes at once and stamp them all at the same time.

Sealing can be a difficult task, but not if you follow this technique. Take a pile of about twenty-five envelopes with flaps open and seal the top one, fold over, and remove it from the pile. If you do this quickly, the excess water will fall on the remaining flaps and you will avoid a mess. Once the pile of envelopes is sealed, press down one more time to ensure a good closure. Separate the envelopes before stacking in a bin or bag so that any remaining moisture will not cause the envelopes to stick together.

When filling orders, have all of your supplies laid out in front of you. Sort the pile of coded labels so that those ordering the same product are all together. Labels for multiple products make an additional pile. First, put the coded label on the proper size packages and then fill all of the packages for the same products at the same time. Double-check the contents of each package and then seal all of the packages at once. Second, follow the procedures for the method of shipping you are using. If you are weighing packages yourself, make sure you use an approved and accurate scale. UPS, FedEx, and other shippers will pick up your packages for a slight additional charge.

Postage and supplies can be costly. If you are unsure of the weight of an envelope you are mailing, have it weighed at the post office. Putting excess postage on envelopes and packages is a waste of money that can add up quickly. There are many techniques you can use to trim postal costs, such as the following:

- Keep your envelope sizes within postal guidelines. There are surcharges for envelopes that are larger, even if they weigh one ounce or less.
- Before printing, weigh the papers and envelope that will comprise your mailing piece. If you are mailing first class, you will have to pay for an additional ounce, even if the weight is only one-tenth of an ounce over. Remember, when printed, the inserts will be slightly heavier. If you are sending your mailings via bulk rate, the postage increases only after you exceed 3.5 ounces.
- Store your printing away from temperature fluctuations. Paper absorbs some of the humidity and dampness that could add to the weight of your mailing piece. To protect against damage from leaks, never store printing directly on a garage floor.
- Address your mail using the U.S. Postal Service recommendations. Addresses should be typewritten and use standard abbreviations. Make sure you use the standardized two-letter state abbreviations.
- Use a computer program that can bar-code your addresses automatically. This will help you qualify for discounts.
- Invest in a professional-quality scale.

PROFIT PROFILE: Multichannel Order Manager

A Software Package to Help You Run Your Business

Your computer can automatically perform many of the tasks involved with running your business when you use a specially designed software system.

Multichannel Order Manager (M.O.M.) helps you track every aspect of an order. Sold modularly, the main system allows you to enter the type and quantity of each product you sell, and keeps an inventory as you enter orders. Vendor records allow purchase orders to be generated when products fall below established low-level limits. The program also calculates shipping charges and payment information, and does invoicing. When you enter advertising key codes, the program will track response rate and profit analysis to help you see where your orders are coming from. Powerful look-up features allow you to use telephone number, last name, zip code, company name, or a special customer number you create to find the record you are looking for. Selectable order-processing options let you control the printing of invoices, packing slips, shipping labels, customer form letters, drop-shipment notices, and shipping manifests.

For more information on M.O.M., contact Dydacomp Development Corp., 11-D Commerce Way, Totowa, NJ 07512; (800) 858-3666. Or visit their website at www.dydacomp.com.

Inventory Control

Let's face it. Without an inventory of products to sell, you do not have a mail order business. Keeping a watchful eye on the products coming in and going out each day is essential. The most efficient way to keep track of inventory is to use one of the mail order management programs. If this is not possible, you will have to keep track of your products or raw materials the old-fashioned way—by counting and writing down the results on a regular basis. Your sales record can also help you determine how much merchandise you have available on the shelf.

Maintaining the right amount of inventory at all times is an art. You don't want to wait until you are almost out of stock before you reorder an item. You need a time cushion to make sure that your products will be available at all times. On the other hand, you don't want to stock too much product, for then a good chunk of your operating expenses will be tied up for too long. Ultimately the amount of inventory you must have on hand will depend on the reliability of your suppliers. If you feel confident that you can get needed delivery quickly, you can wait a little longer before reordering. And here is another reason to develop a good relationship with your suppliers: If they will give you a thirty-, sixty-, or even a ninety-day grace period before you have to pay for the goods, you will have greater use of your money.

When your merchandise is delivered, you need to check the quantity and condition of the shipment. If you have received damaged goods or less than you ordered, you need to have that information right away. Check the number of cartons and examine the merchandise to make sure that it is in good condition.

To maintain a correct inventory, you will need to keep the following records:

- The names of the vendors that are your primary sources and any alternate suppliers.
- The date of the last inventory.
- The quantity at which you must reorder.
- The number of units that are ordered each time.
- The number of units still on hand when a new shipment is received.
- The number of units that have actually been sold, used, or given away each month. If this number goes up and stays up for a few weeks, you may want to order a higher quantity each time.
- The number of units that are on order but not yet received.

Your Partner—The Post Office

As a home-based mail order business owner, you will probably develop a love–hate relationship with the post office. But like it or not, the post office will become an essential part of your business. You can ship packages via UPS, FedEx, or another delivery service, but your direct-mail promotions and orders will be delivered via the U.S. Postal Service (USPS). The post office delivers billions of pieces of mail each year. With so much mail traveling through the system, there are bound to be mistakes. The more you understand postal procedures, the more you can ensure that your mail will be handled properly.

The USPS realizes that it is in competition with independent carriers, e-mail, and fax machines, and welcomes the opportunity to work with small-business mailers. A small business is defined as a company that spends less than $100,000 per year on postage and fees. If you are just starting your business, it pays to ask your local postmaster for the name of the person who is responsible for working with small businesses in your area. When you speak with the designated person, explain your business and the services you need from the post office. He or she will give you the information you need about obtaining permits and recommend ways to reduce postage. Essentially, the higher the volume of your mail and the smaller the geographical area you mail to, the lower your postal rates will be.

Ask to take a tour of mail-processing facilities so that you can see exactly what happens to your mail, especially a bulk mailing. You will begin to understand why the postal service gives discounts to those mailers who do as much preparation as possible before bringing in their mailing. Training classes and seminars are available, as well as video presentations. The USPS also publishes a free newsletter called *Memo to Mailers*. To receive more information about this newsletter or other postal issues, go to www.usps.gov.

Federal Trade Commission's Thirty-Day Mail Order Rule

In an effort to protect the interests of mail order buyers, the Federal Trade Commission passed the Mail Order Rule in 1975. It has since been amended to also include orders placed by telephone, by fax, or online. The rule states that orders should be filled within thirty days of receipt. If you cannot do so, you must state a delivery time on your order form, such as "Please allow six weeks for delivery."

If you realize that an order will not be mailed on time, you are required to let your customer know the shipping date. You must offer a refund and enclose a postage-paid envelope for reply. If the customer does not reply, you may consider that an acceptance. This rule is strictly enforced, and you can receive penalties of up to $10,000 for each violation, so it is important that you comply.

Customer Service

Customer service is everything you do to help your customers place and receive their orders with ease and solve any problems that may occur along the way. Your customers have a right to expect excellent service, and you have the responsibility to provide it. By keeping track of customer compliments and complaints, you will have a way to judge the efficiency of your company.

Even if you make an effort to provide excellent customer service, sooner or later you will get a customer complaint. When speaking with your customer, make sure that you learn the exact nature of the problem and what you are being requested to do to resolve the situation. You should have a written return policy that can guide you. Make sure that you handle complaints quickly and to the customer's satisfaction. If your customer is happy with the result, he or she may continue to order from your company. Everyone knows that it is easier to keep a customer than to find a new one. If you cannot solve a problem, a full refund is in order.

Common Mail-Processing Questions

Q: Should I wait for checks to clear before I ship orders?

A: The answer to this question depends on many different factors. What is the amount of the check? Are your customers interested in quick delivery? Does your competition offer immediate shipping? Do you offer the option of paying by credit card? If those interested in quick delivery can charge their purchases but choose to send a check, then you could delay shipping until the check clears. However, if the amount of the check is not high, and you don't yet offer the credit card option, shipping quickly can earn you customer satisfaction and repeat sales.

Q: What is drop shipping?

A: Drop shipping is a special arrangement you can make with some suppliers or manufacturers. You advertise a product without keeping an inventory. When you receive an order, you send the name and address of your customer and a check for the wholesale price but keep the profit. Drop shipping is one way to limit your up-front expenses when you are starting your business, but you sacrifice complete control over when your customer's order will be shipped.

Q: Is it okay to use form letters to answer customer questions?

A: You can prepare standardized letters that can be used to communicate with your customers, but these letters should be personalized with the customer's name, address, and any other pertinent information. This can be done on your computer. If you are not using a computer, use the letter you have prepared as a guide as you type a letter directly to your customer. Form letters are too impersonal.

Q: With so many postal regulations, how can I possibly learn about all the options and discounts?

A: The postal code consists of thousands of pages of information, and regulations are always changing. This book can only touch on the surface of the information you need to know. The U.S. Postal Service has established one hundred Postal Business Centers in metropolitan areas. They were designed to assist small-business owners like you to understand what is available to them. Check the government pages of your telephone book or call your local post office for the location of the Postal Business Center nearest you. Online, go to www.usps.gov.

11 Growing Pains and Pleasures

The telephone rings all day, the orders are pouring in, and your home-based mail order business is making more money than you ever imagined possible. All of your hard work is paying off, and what could be better than a successful business right in your own home? If this is your dream, watch out. There is a big difference between fantasizing about home business success and actually dealing with the added work, stress, and responsibility that come along with it. If you plan ahead now, you could avoid the pressures and pitfalls that come with business growth.

If you are like most home business owners, your independence is important to you. You enjoy being in control of every aspect of your business and hesitate to delegate any task. In the beginning you are able to take care of all the varied aspects of your business, and that suits you just fine. You follow your own instincts, work hard . . . and pow! Success hits hard and fast, and you are shocked to realize that this increase in business is more than you can handle alone. Few situations can cause so much happiness and misery all at once.

Will It Last?

Before you make any moves, you need to determine if this is a temporary spurt of business or if your business has climbed to a new level of operation that can be sustained. If you feel it is temporary, you can react less dramatically. Success comes in stages and is not always consistent. The saying, "Two steps forward, one step back," is an accurate description of progress in any area. Making plans and goals and accomplishing them one at a time will keep you pointed in the right direction. To help you reevaluate your circumstances, ask yourself these questions:

- What caused the surge in business?
- Is it repeatable?
- Is it sustainable?
- Is it seasonal?
- Will finding additional space and getting help ensure your continued growth, or will the cost cause a downward spiral?

The answers to these questions will help you determine your next step. Are you swamped with work because you received publicity, or is it because your marketing plan is working? Response from publicity will die off, and even if it helps build your house mailing list, you will not stay at this level of business for too long. But if you have discovered excellent placement for your ads or your new catalog is pulling twice the previous response rate, you may have positioned yourself for sustained success.

Before you make any permanent moves, take steps now that will help you in the months and years to come. Put some money in savings to back you up if your cash flow decreases, and don't increase your expenses without serious consideration. Make sure you can cover your commitments if sales return to their previous lower level.

Review your marketing plan. What moves can you make to keep sales up? Should you place new ads or institute a publicity campaign? Is it time to create your website? Seeking new customers is essential, especially when times are good. You also want to keep your existing customers. Even though you are busy, customer service comes first. Regular mailings to your house list of happy customers will keep you in the black.

Your personal traits could also affect your company's ultimate success. You may have made it through the start-up phase of your business by using your instincts and improvising. But as your business grows, improvisation won't work. You have to know what moves to make, and if your business has surpassed your skill level, you could be in trouble. If an employee fails to do his or her job correctly, he or she has to answer to the boss. But when it is the boss (you) who is less than competent, problems can escalate quickly.

It is up to you to realize any shortcomings and confront them. You may have been good at start-up, but managing a larger business takes new and different skills. The transition could be difficult unless you make an honest assessment of your strengths and weaknesses, and redefine your role in the company. If your mail order business is successful because you are an innovative inventor and marketer, you might want to continue doing what you do well and hire someone to actually run the company.

Getting the Help You Need

The day you realize that you cannot handle all of the work that needs to be done in your business will be a turning point. Anticipate that day and be ready for change so your business can move forward on schedule. The decisions you make could affect the profitability of your business and your working conditions. A support team of qualified individuals and companies can greatly enhance your personal talents and skills. There are many choices to think about when you can no longer run your business by yourself, and this chapter will help you consider many of your options.

Outsourcing

If you have too much work to do but would like to avoid hiring employees to work in your home, you can use the services of outside businesses to help you avoid dealing with the daily invasion of privacy and the many legal responsibilities connected with becoming an employer. Other home-based or small firms would welcome your business and could offer very affordable rates.

First, you must decide which tasks you want to handle yourself and which you want to delegate. Second, try to determine if you need temporary help or ongoing assistance. Jobs ranging from bookkeeping to inbound telemarketing to word processing can be handled by independent contractors. Independent contractors are people who offer a service to a number of different companies for compensation, but they are not considered employees. *But be careful:* You cannot hire people to work for you and then call them independent contractors to avoid withholding taxes or to elude the other responsibilities employers must fulfill.

Despite the fact that there is no precise legal definition of an independent contractor, the IRS and state tax agencies have gotten tough, and many small businesses have been required to explain the status of some freelance workers. Here are some of the factors the IRS considers when determining independent contractor status:

- Is the person required to comply with company instructions about when, where, and how the work is done?

- Has he or she been trained by the company?
- Must the person render services personally?
- Does he or she use assistants provided by the company?
- Is the person required to work a set number of hours?
- Does the person work full-time for the company?
- Does the person work on the company premises?
- Must the person work in a prearranged sequence?
- Does the person use company tools and materials?
- Is the person paid by the hour, the week, or the month?

To protect yourself, you can prepare a written "Work for Hire" agreement that will specify your working relationship. Commerce Clearing House publishes: *Independent Contractor or Employee? Guide to Resolving the Question* by Neil Ringques, JD, CPA ($39). To order, call (800) 248-3248.

Using Temporary-Help Services

Hiring an employee is a big step; however, employees hired through a temporary-help agency could be your answer right now. Temporary helpers are available in almost every position. Many employees who have been victims of downsizing have gone to work as temporaries. More than one million people are temporary employees, and many are highly skilled.

Temporary help is appealing to home-based business owners because the agencies do all of the screening and paperwork. Help is available from clerical to word processing, bookkeeping to marketing—whatever help you need, the right temporary agency could help. Using temporary help can also be a good dress rehearsal for hiring employees. You can see what it is like working with others in your home and test your skill as a manager. To find temporary-help agencies, look in the Yellow Pages under Employment Contractors—Temporary. Look for agencies that are members of the National Association of Temporary Services (NATS).

Hiring A Virtual Assistant

A virtual assistant (VA) can be the perfect answer for a mail order business owner that needs help with any aspect of his business. Working in her own office located anywhere in the world, a VA can perform any task you need. You can develop a relationship with one VA or use a variety of virtual assistants with different specialties.

Because you will most likely pay your VA on an assignment-by-assignment basis, you will not have to commit to a long-term relationship or provide any benefits.

You might want a virtual assistant who does your administrative work so that you have more time for doing more important tasks. Or, you can hire a virtual assistant who specializes in creating and maintaining websites, creating e-books, writing blog posts, or social networking. All of your interaction with a virtual assistant will be online or by telephone, which will help you keep your privacy. A virtual assistant can also save you money because she will use her own equipment.

Although virtual assistants can be found all over the world, it can be more convenient if the ones you choose are in the same time zone as you are. This will allow you to communicate easily during business hours. How do you find the right VA for you? Most virtual assistants have their own websites. Just go to a search engine and type in "virtual assistant" plus the keywords for the type of work you need done.

Choosing a Backup Team

They aren't employees, and many entrepreneurs avoid them, but there are three types of professionals that can help you manage your growing business: an accountant, an attorney, and a banker. You may think that you don't need the help of these professionals. Why hire a CPA or a lawyer? It will cost too much money. And developing a relationship with a banker is a waste of time. The fact is, you will probably make some expensive mistakes if you don't occasionally consult these and other professionals. There are ways, however, that you can get expert input from them without breaking the bank. Following the advice of trusted advisers will help you cope with the growth of your business and make the right moves.

A banker can help you evaluate your business plan and tell you if you will have enough capital for expansion. He or she can also refer you to the right accountant and even suggest an attorney. Does it make sense to develop a relationship with a banker if you are not seeking a loan? Sure. Getting a banker on your side can never hurt. And when your business takes off, he or she may be ready to fund your growth. So find a banker who is interested in your business and take him or her to lunch.

An accountant is a vital member of your team. You need someone you can trust with the intimate financial details of your business, someone who can take care of tax matters and help you prepare necessary reports. Your accountant will help you change your record-keeping system as your business grows. If you decide to hire employees, your accountant will help you handle your responsibilities as an employer and set up your employee benefits plan.

An attorney who is well versed in small-business matters will also be an asset to your business. In addition to all legal matters, your attorney can be an adviser who will help you make the right connections and take the right steps as your business grows. If your attorney has worked with other small companies, he or she will have had a firsthand look at the successful and not so successful moves other business owners have made.

Where should you look to find the right members for your backup team? You have to decide if you want to go to a large firm or use a small, independent company. Will it serve any purpose in your profession to be represented by a large firm with a strong reputation? Do you feel comfortable in a corporate atmosphere, or do you prefer to work with others who are much like you? Smaller firms or individual practitioners will probably provide more personalized service, but larger firms may have a greater variety of experts on hand. As a female entrepreneur, I prefer to deal with other women. I realize that men possess all the necessary qualifications, but I just feel more comfortable working with women advisers. The people you choose should reflect your own personal preferences and needs.

There are ways to save money when seeking advice from your backup team. Consider the following tips before you seek advice.

- Do your homework and prepare for your meeting. Presenting organized records and papers will save time, and time is money.
- Don't call each time you have a question; instead, save some questions and then make one telephone call.
- Provide your advisers with all of your business's printed materials and make sure that they have a clear picture of your business and how it is run. Then keep your advisers updated as time goes on.
- Don't put up with unacceptable service. If you are unhappy, say so or look for another adviser.

Using a Fulfillment Center

If you have limited space and don't like to handle details, you could consider hiring a company to take your orders and fill them. There are fulfillment houses that handle everything from order taking to shipping to customer service. When you hire a fulfillment house, all of your warehouse space and a lot of the drudge work associated with running a home-based mail order business will magically disappear from your home.

Because most mail order businesses have peaks and valleys in their sales volume, it is not practical to keep a full staff all year. That is why many mail order businesses do not handle their own order fulfillment. If this sounds like a good solution for you, you need to sort through the services available and choose the fulfillment company that is right for you. The following are some guidelines to help you evaluate:

- *What services are offered?* Do they handle all the services you require?
- *During what hours do they take telephone orders?* You want the inbound telemarketing to be available at least during business hours across the country. That means a West Coast company should take calls beginning at 6:00 a.m. to accommodate the East Coast. East Coast companies should take calls until at least 8:00 p.m., which is 5:00 p.m. in the West.
- *Can they take credit card orders using your merchant account?* If you are using their credit card processing, what percentage rates will they charge?
- *How will you be charged for their services?* Some companies charge a percentage of the gross sales, usually ranging between 5 and 20 percent. Others may charge by the minute or the job done. You can expect a minimum charge.

You should check out the companies you are considering as much as possible. Try placing an order to evaluate their customer service and speed of delivery. If possible, make an on-site visit, then check references. It is especially important to speak with other companies using their services. Your fulfillment company should appear to be a part of your company to the customer who calls and places an order. To accomplish this you should have the ability to speak with and train their people. There are many fulfillment companies operating nationwide. A brief listing appears in the appendix.

Should You Take on a Partner?

Taking on a partner could be the answer you are searching for—or maybe not. If you choose someone who has different but complementary skills, the division of work will be easy to accomplish. If you love marketing and hate the day-to-day details of operating your business, a detail person could be a good choice for a partnership. A person who has work space available may be able to move part of the business out of your home and solve your space problems. The capital a partner brings into the business could help you buy needed equipment and step up your promotional efforts.

Before you begin your search for the perfect partner, a word of caution. Partnerships are complicated and often fail. The person you choose needs to have a clearly defined role in the business and expectations that match yours. If a partnership seems like the right answer for you, proceed slowly and make sure that you have a written agreement. You could be headed for legal or professional complications. If your partner gets into legal trouble, you could also be liable.

Although a partnership agreement is not required by law, smart partners will sign one and include the following points:

- One or two paragraphs describing the business and its goals.
- An accounting of how much each partner will contribute in cash, property, or labor.
- Details on how the profits will be split.
- Specifications for how much and how often money can be withdrawn for the business.
- Arrangements for what happens to the business when one partner dies, leaves, or cannot continue working in the business. Each partner should have approval before any transfer can be made.
- Specifications of the financial and legal powers and responsibilities of each partner.

Husbands and Wives as Business Partners

When your partner is your spouse, you may think that your business relationship will be a natural extension of your marriage. But unless you create clear boundaries between your work and family life, you could be headed for trouble. Marriage partners expect unconditional love, but business partners must produce good work before recognition occurs. This change of attitude could cause conflict. Business partnerships between husbands and wives can and do work, but there are the following factors to consider before you take the plunge:

- Can you separate business and personal matters? It is important to keep the business going, even when your home life is not ideal.

- Do you recognize and admire each other's weaknesses and skills? Have you developed a successful system for decision making in your personal life, or do you argue over minor details?
- Do you have good communication skills in all areas?
- Do you share a vision for the company instead of working just to make money?
- Will your business roles and home responsibilities be equitably divided?

Married couples have to expect blurred boundaries between work and family, especially when the business is home-based. If you are both working at home, who will pick up the kids? Who will cook dinner? Discussing all the potential problems before working as partners will help avoid trouble.

Hiring Employees

If the options mentioned so far are not appropriate for your situation, you will have to consider becoming an employer. This is a step that many home-based business owners avoid. Hiring employees changes everything about your business. Sure, it can put you on the road to success. But your time, your work space, and your operating procedures are no longer your own.

Before you begin the hiring process, take the time to determine your state's laws and regulations, and learn the federal requirements. You must learn about Social Security and taxes to be withheld from paychecks, federal and state unemployment taxes, disability insurance, and safety regulations. Good employers also provide some kind of health insurance, paid holidays, vacations, sick leave, and other fringe benefits.

If you think you can handle all of these responsibilities and paperwork, you are ready to begin your search for the right employee. You must be very careful when searching for the right person to work in your home. Before you even invite someone to your home for an interview, ask for a résumé with references you can check. When meeting for the first time, you might want to consider meeting in a neutral place, such as a restaurant.

Finding the right employee may not be easy. Interviewing is an art that must be learned. To elicit the most telling responses, you have to ask the right questions. You can write down a job description to help you focus on the types of skills your potential employee must possess, but remember that qualifications are not your only consideration. You also need to feel comfortable with the people who will be working in your home. In a sense, the employees of your home-based business will become part of your family.

Remember, you cannot discriminate when hiring employees. If you make the wrong moves, you could be sued. It is illegal to ask certain questions, such as the applicant's age or pregnancy plans.

Other points to consider when hiring include the following:

- Will your neighbors be upset when they see employees reporting to work every day, causing zoning complaints?
- Can your employees telecommute so that they won't have to work on your premises?
- Will the people you hire make a valuable contribution to your business? If they can't increase your profits enough at least to cover their salaries, it may not be worth the trouble.

Hiring Friends and Family

Because you want to feel comfortable with the people you work with, you may decide that friends and family would be good employees. You may be right . . . but you may be wrong. If you are unhappy with the work of an employee who is also someone close to you, firing that employee could cause you to lose a friendship or close family tie, along with an incompetent worker.

Before you invite a friend or family member to become an employee, make sure you clearly define the position that person will have in your business. Include the salary, job duties, and potential for advancement. If long hours are required, say so up front. If the person doesn't have the required skills or experience or a checkable employment history, there is nothing to guarantee that there will be an improvement under your employ. Will he or she be willing to take direction or orders from you? A written preemployment agreement defining your working relationship can help.

Creating Space

If you are committed to working at home no matter what the cost, you might have to move or add on to your existing residence. Before you break down the walls or call the real estate agent, analyze the existing space in your home. Do you have an attic, a garage, or a basement you could convert or a porch or patio that could be enclosed? Taking full advantage of the available space in your home is certainly easier and less expensive than constructing an addition or even building a separate structure on your property. Think creatively: A mobile office (such as those used on construction sites) or a large tent or storage shed could relieve some of your space pressure. Apartment dwellers could consider renting a nearby apartment in the same building instead of moving to a house. Here are some more strategies to consider.

Two for the Money

Renting an outside office can help you cope and save your at-home career. You can use your outside office as a work space for your employees, to receive mail and telephone calls, accept large deliveries, house large equipment, or meet with clients. A storefront would give you the opportunity to sell to walk-in traffic if that is one of your goals. Fax machines and computer modems can help you pass information back and forth between your outside office and your home office. In a sense you would be telecommuting to your own business. At least one trustworthy employee is a key ingredient for making this arrangement work.

Renting or buying a freestanding building with commercial space or a storefront with living quarters upstairs is another option. In effect the business would be the main focus, and your living quarters would take up less space.

Rent Time

You could arrange to rent the facilities of larger, better-equipped companies during off-hours. An outside bakery meets all health regulations and has professional equipment. You could hire your own printer and rent time using a local printer's press at night. Renting time in a workshop will give you access to professional tools and prevent you from bothering your neighbors with the noise of machinery. Need a meeting room away from home? You could consider renting a hotel room or the conference room in a local office. Commercial warehouse space is also available if you need additional storage space for your stock.

Adding On

Building codes require a permit to add on to or substantially alter your residence. You will want your addition to add value to your house. When you sell it, the new owners may not want a home office, so you should design your addition so that it can be adapted for living space. An architect or building contractor should be consulted when adding load-bearing walls.

Planning your home office addition will consist of four separate steps:

1. Take an inventory of the equipment and furniture that you already own.
2. Determine the function and concept for the new space.
3. Design your new office and plan the furniture and equipment locations.
4. Implement your plans.

Home additions can be costly, and it would be wise to determine if it is economically feasible before you begin. Consider the following points:

- What will be the total cost of the space, added equipment, and furnishings? Can you afford to finance it, and do you consider it an investment or an expense?
- Will your house increase in value equal to the amount you spend on the addition? Don't forget to factor in the interest on a loan or lost interest from savings.
- What is your goal for the addition? More space? A more pleasant work environment?
- Will the increased space increase income?
- While construction is taking place, you will not have the use of the space. Where will you work, and will there be costs involved?

Don't forget to include proper lighting, wall bookcases for product storage, adequate space to move around, and good security for doors and windows. A separate entrance, bathroom, and space for a small refrigerator and microwave would make the room self-sufficient and suitable for meeting with clients.

Pay your contractor in installments that are geared to levels of completion. The largest payment should be the final one, giving the contractor the incentive to complete the job in a timely manner.

Moving Out

If you need more space than an addition can give you, it might be time to purchase a larger home. Your choice should have more room than you anticipate needing now to avoid another move in the future. Is there room for separate offices so that you don't have to share space with employees? Can you build specialized storage space? A two-family home may be a good choice if you use one apartment for living and the other for your business.

Should You Leave the Nest?

If you are trying to decide whether it is time to move your business out of your home, you can only look inside yourself for the answer. This is a very personal decision that cannot be dictated by tradition. There are many large corporations, such as Apple Computer, that had to leave their home-based beginnings to realize their full potential. But maybe you would prefer to maintain the status quo instead of transforming your home-based operation into a mega mail order concern.

If you are considering moving out, don't make the move under pressure or in a panic situation. You need to plan every detail and be sure that your growth will cover your increased expenses through the long haul. One home-based mail order business owner who made the move advises, "If you decide to move out, be prepared to begin a new phase of your business. It will never be the same again."

Two home-based mail order business owners, Steve and Sandy F., would never voluntarily move their business out of their home. They started their desktop booklet-publishing business in a barn on their farm in upstate New York because they love the lifestyle. They have plenty of room for their computers, laser printers, and book storage, and most of their business is done through the mail. They take turns caring for their two young children and cherish the flexibility a home business affords them. When the opportunity to write and publish a monthly newsletter for a big account came along, the added work put pressure on them, and they had to hire someone to help watch their children. They were making more money, but they weren't happy with the changes in their daily routine. So Steve and Sandy made the decision to scale back and referred the new account to another local business. They were not willing to give up the laid-back lifestyle that was more important to them than increased income. "We've had the best of both worlds," explains Steve. "That's hard to give up at any price."

Common Business Expansion Questions

Q: I need help in my mail order business but fear hiring employees. I'm not afraid of working with others in my home, but I'm afraid of all the paperwork and legal obligations. Exactly what would I have to do?

A: When you hire employees, they are subject to the Fair Labor Standards Act of 1938. The FLSA contains guidelines regarding minimum wage, overtime, equal pay, child labor, and more. The Department of Labor administers the law. Your employees' wages are also subject to tax withholding, reporting, and depositing by federal, state, and local tax authorities.

You must comply with the hourly minimum-wage standards set by local and state guidelines. If your employees qualify for overtime pay, time-and-a-half must be paid for all hours worked in excess of forty per week. Social Security, Medicare, and some state taxes also apply. Employers also have to pay federal unemployment tax and state unemployment tax for each employee.

You need to have an Employer Identification Number before you can withhold taxes. Reports also have to be made to the IRS, and you must fill out state tax forms too. An IRS Form W-2, Wage and Tax Statement, must be issued to the employee before January 31 each year.

If all this seems too complicated, you can contract with a payroll service, an employee leasing service, or an accounting firm to handle these details for you.

Q: I have hired my first employees and now I want to make sure that my mail order business will continue to operate using my guidelines. Besides watching over my employees, how can I make this happen?

A: An operations manual will give your employees a standardized listing of the company's operations, objectives, and approved environment. Having a manual will give your employees a written, single source to interpret lines of authority and responsibilities. You can also give guidelines for decision-making and management style while providing a training tool for employees. There are computer programs available that can assist you in writing your employee manual.

Final Thoughts

I hope that I have delivered on my promises, just as all mail order business owners should. My goal in writing this book was to show you that owning a home-based mail order business is a dream that can come true for anyone who wants to learn proven techniques and work hard.

Sometimes, beginning is the hardest part. If you are waiting for the most convenient time, enough money to invest, or the perfect business idea, you will only continue to wait. Even though we all have the potential to become exactly what we would like to be, fear often causes us to lock our talents and creativity away. Now is the time to make the decision to reach for your dreams, to set your abilities free and let yourself become everything you would like to be. Unless you take that first step, your neglected dreams will simply fade away.

What should that first step be? The best place to begin is at the end of this book. Use the appendix to help you do further research on all aspects of running a home-based mail order business. Read everything you can, and speak with as many people as possible to get ideas and inspiration. But don't stop there. Go online and begin to make contacts and do further research by typing your keywords into a search engine like Google.

Even if you are not ready for a full-time commitment, get started. Keep a notebook of your ideas and pertinent information. Find great products and determine your target market. Research that market to determine how you will promote your products. Analyze your competition. Adopt and improve on their strong points and correct any weaknesses.

Choose a time that will be convenient and make a habit of working on your business at that time each day of your work week. Form some preliminary goals and create step-by-step plans for meeting each of them by a certain date. Develop a master "to-do" list and use it to schedule your daily business activities. Name your business and have stationery and business cards printed. Register a domain name and get an e-mail address with your business name.

Before long, you will feel a change come over you. Your business will begin to take on a life of its own and evolve in ways you did not anticipate. You will get that special feeling only a true entrepreneur feels when you know that you are making the right moves and it is only a matter of time until success is yours. It is that delicious feeling of anticipation that makes business start-up so exciting.

I have tried to inform and inspire you. Keep this book nearby to help you get over the rough spots, and don't forget to let me know about your achievements. You could be featured in my next book or magazine article. And remember, live links to the resources in this book are available at: www.HomeWorkingMom.com/for-readers-of-how-to-start-a-home-based-mail-order-business. The next step—your first step—is up to you. Make this the day you begin.

Appendix A: Mail Order Glossary

Active customer: Any mail order buyer who has ordered within the last twelve months.

Address correction requested: An instruction a mailer puts on an outgoing letter asking the postal service to supply the new address if an addressee has moved. The mailing piece is returned with the new address indicated. There is no fee for first-class mail. ACR can be used to update a mailing list.

Add-on service: Consumers can contact the Direct Marketing Association to request being added to particular mailing lists.

Additions: New names that have been added to a mailing list.

Advertising rate card: Printed information that details advertising cost, ad sizes, and production details for potential advertisers.

Agency discount: The discount or commission that an advertising agency receives for placing an ad.

Airtime: The amount of time available for a television or radio ad.

Assigned mailing dates: Dates specified for mailing to a rented list.

Audience: The number of people who will have the opportunity to see a specific promotion or advertisement.

Augmentation: Adding information to one mailing list from another mailing list.

Back-end marketing: Selling a product or service to someone who is already your customer.

Bar code: A series of vertical bars that represent numbers of a delivery point and a zip code. Bar codes help speed mail, because they can be read by high-speed machinery. Mailers receive discounts if their mail is bar coded.

Bill enclosure: Promotional piece that is added to the envelope when a bill is sent out.

Bingo card: A promotional reply card that is inserted in a publication.

Brochure: A pamphlet that is designed and produced with the purpose of promoting a product or service.

Body copy: The main portion of the written text in press releases or advertisements.

Bounce-back: An offer put inside the package of a fulfilled order. It encourages the buyer to make another purchase.

Bulk mail: Third-class mail. The mailer presorts a minimum of 200 pieces of identical mail and receives a discounted postage rate. Bulk mail takes approximately two weeks to be delivered. A yearly fee is charged in addition to postage.

Bullet: A bold dot used for emphasis. Usually placed in front of important features or sentences.

Business-reply card (or envelope): A card or envelope provided to prospective customers enabling them to mail information requests or orders without having to pay postage. The mail order company must pay the postage plus additional fees upon receipt.

Call to action: Encouraging the audience to react appropriately to a marketing effort.

Card deck: Advertisements from a variety of businesses that are printed on small cards, packaged together, and mailed to magazine subscribers or other consumers with common interests or needs.

Classified advertisement: Small-space advertising that is placed in columns in designated areas of publications.

Clip art: Photos and drawings that can be purchased by the public for use in advertising.

COD: Cash on delivery. A buyer pays for an ordered product plus an additional charge when delivery is received.

Cold list: A list of prospects that has not been mailed to or tested.

Collate: To assemble pages or other elements of a mailing in the correct sequence.

Communications software: A program that allows a computer and modem to give you access to a bulletin board or an online service.

Compiled list: A mailing list comprising names taken from telephone directories, other directories, and public records. The compiler owns the list and can rent it for one-time use or lease it for unlimited use.

Conversion rate: The percentage of direct mail recipients who become buyers.

Copy: Words or text written for publication, broadcast, or production.

Co-op mailing: Two or more offers from individual advertisers that share the cost of a mailing.

CPM: Cost per thousand. Used when pricing advertising.

CPO: Cost per order. A mathematical formula that divides the total cost of a mailing or advertisement by the total resulting orders received.

Creative: The creative aspects of a catalog or advertisement including the design, copywriting, and photos or illustrations.

Database: A computerized compilation of related information designed for ease of use and retrieval.

Database marketing: The analysis of customer data used to target specific market segments.

Data card: A card that specifies the details of a mailing list such as cost per thousand and demographics.

DBA (doing business as): A registered business name that is different from that of the business owner (e.g., John Smith DBA Home Direct Marketing).

Decision maker: The person at an address who has the ability to authorize an order.

Decoy (or seed) names: Names added to a rented mailing list by the owner to help ascertain if the list is being used more times than agreed upon.

Deliverability: The percentage of a rented list that can be delivered by third-class mail.

Demographics: The age, income, location, education, family size, and so on that are shared by a group of people who are on a list or in a target market.

Direct mail: Promotional material sent through the mail to a targeted list of potential customers.

Direct marketing: Includes direct mail and most other media. It is marketing that seeks an immediate response (a request for information, an order, and so on) that can be tested and tracked. Also called direct-response marketing.

Discretionary income: Income 30 percent greater than the local cost of living plus taxes that is available to spend on luxuries or other nonessential purchases. Direct marketers often choose households with high discretionary income, because they can afford to make purchases.

Dollar value per order: The average monetary value of purchases for each order received as a result of a mailing. The gross revenue is divided by the number of orders.

Doubling day: Approximately one week after a first class mailing when one-half of the responses will have been received.

Download: Transferring data from one source to another (e.g., from a disk into a computer or from a computer into a printer).

Drop shipment: Merchandise purchased through a catalog or other direct-response offer that is mailed directly to the customer from the manufacturer. The direct marketer collects paid orders from the customer and then forwards names and wholesale payment to the product source for shipment.

Drop day: The day a mailing is entered into the postal system.

Dupe elimination: Eliminating duplicate names from a mailing list or group of mailing lists that have been merged.

E-mail: Electronic mail. Messages sent almost instantaneously from one computer user to another via modem.

Enhanced fax: Any use of a fax machine other than basic transmission.

Envelope stuffers: Printed promotional material that can be placed into the envelopes of other mailers.

External list: A list that comes from an outside source.

Fax broadcasting: Personalized documents faxed to a large group of people at one time.

Fax marketing: The use of a fax machine to sell a product or service, or provide customer support.

Fax-on-demand: Marketing materials faxed in response to a customer's call for information.

Four color: Artwork that is produced in full color.

Fulfillment: Sending information requested or products ordered.

Gross income: The total amount of income before expenses have been deducted.

Hard copy: Information from a computer that has been printed out on paper.

Hotline: A mailing list's most recent buyers, usually within the last month.

House mailing list: The people who have requested information or actually placed an order with a business. A business's house list will always produce the highest response rate.

Inbound telemarketing: Taking information requests and orders from customers responding to a marketing effort.

Independent contractor: An individual who offers a service to a number of different companies for compensation. An independent contractor is not considered an employee, making payroll taxes or other employee paperwork unnecessary.

Indicia: The permit imprint preprinted in the upper right-hand corner of an envelope that substitutes for a stamp. It indicates that postage has been paid.

Inquiry: A request for information or a catalog. Does not include an order.

Interactive voice response (IVR): Customers use the buttons on their Touch-Tone telephones to respond to prerecorded or digitally created instructions.

Internet: A network of networks. Originally a communications system designed to link universities engaged in defense research and the U.S. Department of Defense. Today it has expanded to include organizations across the world. Access is gained through a service provider, such as America Online or a local provider.

ISO (independent sales organization): A company that offers merchant credit card processing services. Can refer to any distributor that buys products and services and resells them at a profit.

Key code: Using letters or numbers on an order form or within the return address to indicate the particular marketing effort that was the source of the inquiry or order.

Lead generation: The result of an ad or other promotional device that attracted requests for product information. Used to identify potential customers. Also called a "hand-raiser."

Logo: A graphic representation of your business.

Mailing-list broker: A person or organization that rents mailing lists to users and sometimes manages the lists for the owners.

Mail monitor: A company that keeps track of your mail delivery and ensures that your list is not used by unauthorized parties.

Marketing: Everything a company does to promote products or services to a defined group of people.

Market segmentation: A division of a group of people using various criteria (age, gender, income, and so on) to pinpoint a specific target market.

Media: Television, radio, printed materials—all methods of communication.

Media kit: A folder of information describing a particular advertising medium, used for the purpose of evaluating the advertising value. A media kit usually contains data on the readership or viewers, circulation, and advertising rates.

Media mix: The combination of various media, such as magazines, television, and newspapers that will effectively reach your target audience.

Megabyte (MB): A unit of measurement for disk space on a computer.

Multimedia: Providing information by using a combination of audio, video, text, and graphics.

Net income: Gross income minus expenses. Your net income is your profit.

Network: A connection for the purpose of communication. Refers to computers or other electronic devices. The Internet is a network of networks—the biggest one in the world.

Niche market: A small segment of a target market that has very specialized interests and needs. Niche marketing can produce a higher percentage of response than marketing to an entire target market.

One-call fax-on-demand: Requested marketing materials are transmitted to a customer who places a call from a fax machine. The marketer does not have to call back to relay material.

Outbound telemarketing: Sales representatives call potential customers to sell a product or service.

Overlay: Adding additional database fields (age, gender, etc.) to an existing database to help target a market.

Partnership: Two or more individuals or entities who agree to contribute skills, money, and so forth to a business and share in the profits, losses, and management.

Piggybacking: Putting your product in another company's catalog.

Premium: A gift offered to potential customers as an incentive to make a purchase.

Press release: A news story or announcement that is mailed to the media in the hope that the information will be disseminated to the public.

Prospect: A person with the ability and desire to purchase a product or service.

Public relations: Efforts a company makes to create a positive image of the company and its products with the public.

RAM (random access memory): The temporary memory a computer uses to process work. When the computer is turned off, the contents of RAM are lost.

Relationship marketing: A method of marketing that pays special attention to the individual customer.

Response rate: The percentage of response received from a marketing effort (e.g., a mailing of 1,000 pieces that produced ten orders would have a 1 percent response rate).

Self-employment tax: Social Security and Medicaid tax, which self-employed individuals must pay.

Self-mailer: A direct-mail promotion that can be folded over so no envelope is required for mailing.

Service bureau: A company that provides inbound and outbound telemarketing. It can also fulfill orders and send marketing materials.

Sole proprietorship: A business that is owned by one person. A sole proprietor is personally liable for all business debts and can reap all of the profits from the business.

Target audience: The people who will be most likely to purchase your product or service.

Telemarketing: Selling a product or service over the telephone.

Test marketing: A small-scale introduction of a new product or service to determine how it will be received by its target market. Results allow refinement before the product is offered on a full scale.

Toll-free telephone number: A telephone number beginning with 800, 877, 866, or 888 that is paid for by the marketer, not the customer.

Two-step promotion: A classified ad or other advertisement that offers free information about a business to potential customers. Those requesting information are sent promotional materials, and their names are put on the business's house mailing list.

Appendix B: Internet Glossary

Ad views: The number of times a banner ad is clicked on and viewed by a visitor to a website. Also called click-throughs.

Affiliate programs: A revenue-sharing arrangement between an online advertiser and an e-commerce company. Payment is based on performance and is usually a percentage of the profit. Affiliate payments can also be based on the number of sales, clicks, or registrations that are referred.

ASCII: American Standard Code for Information Interchange. A system that assigns numeric codes for every upper and lowercase letter of the alphabet and punctuation marks, allowing any computer to communicate with another.

Autoresponder: An e-mail system that automates replies to inquirers.

Banner ad: A graphic image used to attract interest on a website. When selected, the viewer is taken to the advertiser's website.

Baud rate: A measurement of how fast modems and fax machines transfer data.

Blog: Short for Weblog, a website where the blog's owner, called a blogger, makes entries, similar to a journal or a diary. Blogs can be on any topic and are often used to substitute for a website.

Bookmark: A way to cause your computer to remember a website. While viewing the website, choose "bookmark" at the top of your browser.

Browser: Software that allows Internet users to view websites.

Chat: A forum that allows Internet users to communicate in real time.

Cyberspace: A term that describes the online world. The term was first used in a science-fiction book called *Neuromancer* by William Gibson. It refers to the non-physical space where people networking by computer and modem are interacting.

Digital products: Products that are delivered electronically.

Domain name: A set of characters used as an address for a website. Also called a URL or website address.

Download: The transfer of a file from one computer to another.

E-book: A book that is published without paper and can be read on a computer or other digital device.

E-mail: Electronic mail. Sending and receiving written messages on the Internet.

E-zine: Online magazine or newsletter, usually distributed by e-mail.

FAQ: Frequently asked question.

Forums: Places on the Web for holding discussions on a variety of topics.

FTP: File transfer protocol. Enables the transfer of files over the Internet.

Hit: The recorded visit to a website. The number of hits indicates the number of times that a site has been visited.

Home page: The first page of a website. Also called the index page.

Host: A computer that allows other computers to access its files. Every website has a host.

HTML: HyperText Markup Language. A system that is used to code Web page documents that allows Web pages to be viewed by Web browsers.

Hypertext: The code that allows you to click on a word or graphic that is linked to another place on the page, in the website, or in another website.

Internet: A vast collection of interconnected networks.

InterNIC: The organization that supplies domain names.

ISP: Internet Service Provider. A company that provides users access to the Internet.

JPEG: Pronounced "jay peg." The most common type of image used online.

JV: Joint venture. When noncompeting but complementary websites do cross promotions.

Keyword: A term one types into a search engine to find information. Keywords are also used to attract search engines to information online.

Link: A connection between two websites.

Modem: A device that allows computers and other electronic devices to communicate. It converts data so that it can be transmitted and received over telephone lines into files your computer can read.

Online: Communication between computers or people operating computers. You are online when you are using a modem to communicate.

Opt-in: When a prospective customer gives permission to receive marketing material and other information via e-mail.

Pay-per-click: A method of advertising on a search engine. The advertiser is charged each time a visitor clicks on the ad.

PDF: A file format for documents. E-books are usually delivered in PDF format, which allows them to be instantly downloaded.

PPC advertising: Pay Per Click advertising. The advertiser pays a previously agreed-upon amount each time someone clicks on their ad online.

RSS: Really Simple Syndication. The format used for syndicating information online.

Search engine: An online database of Internet sites that allows Internet users to locate subjects of interest.

SEO: Search Engine Optimization. The process of using keywords to generate traffic from search engines to a website.

Service provider: A service that provides a connection between individuals and the Internet.

Spamming: Unethical, unsolicited, and/or unwanted commercial messages sent via e-mail.

Upload: Using a modem to put a file onto the Internet for others to use.

Website: A collection of files consisting of text and graphics that can be found online under one domain name.

URL: Uniform Resource Locator. Another term for a domain name.

Viral marketing: When information is passed quickly from person to person online; for example, a video viewed by millions on YouTube.

www: World Wide Web.

Appendix C: Resources

What is powerful, portable, and ready to help you succeed in your home business? The simple answer is information. The right book, the targeted newsletter, the right organization or website can provide that valuable piece of information that you need to succeed. Knowledge is power; information is empowering. It is exciting to realize that you have the ability to learn anything and everything you need to know by taking advantage of the right information sources. You are in control.

An information source or business tool doesn't have to have the words "mail order" or "home business" in its title to make it valuable to you. Anything designed for small business can be of help to home business owners. Search online booksellers such as Amazon.com, under keywords such as home business, Internet, marketing, online business, small business, and your product category. You should explore your library and bookstore regularly to discover what's new and available to you. Cruise through the aisles of your computer software store or go online, and you will expand your mind and gain a world of help for your business.

Your future is in your hands. To get you started, use the following list of information sources. Resources are listed by chapter with some added recommended reading. Live links to websites and updated information can also be found on www.HomeWorkingMom.com/for-readers-of-how-to-start-a-home-based-mail-order-business.

01 The Magic of Mail Order

National Mail Order Association
2807 Polk St., NE
Minneapolis, MN 55418
(612) 788-1673
www.nmoa.org

Recommended Reading

Start Your Own Mail Order Business: Your Step-by-Step Guide to Success
Entrepreneur Press and Rich Mintzer
Entrepreneur Media, Inc.

02 Managing Mail Order at Home

HomeWorkingMom.com

Recommended Reading

500 Solutions for Working at Home
Anna G. Canizares
Rizzoli Universe Promotional Books

The Smarter Home Office: 8 Simple Steps To Increase Your Income, Inspiration, and Comfort
Linda Varone
Great Meadows Publishing

03 Perfectly Painless Business Planning

Merchant Warehouse
To get a credit card merchant account with no application fee, no set-up fee, and no contracts or cancellation/termination fee either call (866) 761-5531 or go to www.MerchantWarehouse.com/mailorderbusiness.

Recommended Reading

Business Plan Kit for Dummies
Steven D. Peterson, Peter E. Jaret, and Barbara Findlay Schenck
For Dummies

Home Business Tax Deductions: Keep What You Earn, 6th edition
Stephen Fishman
Nolo

Patent, Copyright, & Trademark: An Intellectual Property Desk Reference, 10th edition
Stephen Stim
Nolo

Start Your Own Business: The Only Start-Up Book You'll Ever Need, 5th edition
Entrepreneur Press
Entrepreneur Press

Trademark: Legal Care For Your Business & Product Name, 7th edition
Stephen Elias, and Richard Stim
Nolo

04 Creating No-Fail Direct Mail

The Direct Marketing Association
1120 Avenue of the Americas
New York, NY 10036
(212) 768-7277
www.the-dma.org

Who's Mailing What!
Direct Mail Competitive Intelligence Archive
www.whosmailingwhat.com

Recommended Reading

Open Me Now: Direct Mail Envelopes That Work . . . and Those That Don't, 2nd edition
Herschell Gordon Lewis
Racom Communications and Direct Marketing Association

Words That Sell, 2nd edition
Richard Bayan
McGraw-Hill

05 Mail Order Marketing Basics

Distribute a Press Release Online

BusinessWire.com

Free-Press-Release.com

PRWeb.com

PRNewswire.com

Sell on TV Shopping Networks

Home Shopping Network
New Business Development
1 HSN Drive
St. Petersburg, FL 33729
www.hsn.com

QVC Studio Park
Vendor Relations Department
Mail Stop #0128
1200 Wilson Drive
Westchester, PA 19380
www.vendor.studiopark.com/submit.asp

Recommended Reading

The Copywriter's Handbook, 3rd edition
Robert Bly
Holt Paperbacks

The New Rules of Marketing & PR: How to Use Social Media, Blogs, News Releases, Online Video, and Viral Marketing to Reach Buyers, 2nd edition
David Meerman Scott
Wiley

Outrageous Advertising That's Outrageously Successful: Created for the 99% of Small Business Owners Who Are Dissatisfied with the Results They Get
Bill Glazer and Dan Kennedy
Morgan James Publishing

06 Mail Order Marketing Tools

Recommended Reading

The Encyclopedia of Business Letters, Faxes, and Emails: Features Hundreds of Model Letters, Faxes and Emails to Give Your Business Writing the Attention It Deserves
Robert Bly and Regina Anne Kelly
Career Press

The Truth About Email Marketing
Simms Jenkins
FT Press

Facebook Marketing: An Hour a Day
Chris Treadaway and Mari Smith
Sybex

Social Media Marketing: An Hour a Day
Dave Evans and Susan Bratton
Sybox

Twitter Marketing: Promote Yourself and Your Business on Earth's Hottest Social Network
Steve Weber
Weber Books

07 Selling Your Products Online

Domain Name Registration, Web Hosting, and WordPress

WonderfulWebsiteStore.com

Create Your Own Website

Buildit.Sitesell.com/dreamscometrue3.html

StirSite.com

Recommended Reading

Building a Web Site for Dummies, 4th edition
David A. Crowder
For Dummies

Inbound Marketing: Get Found Using Google, Social Media, and Blogs
Brian Halligan, Dharmesh Shah, David Meerman
Wiley

KaChing: How to Run an Online Business that Pays and Pays
Joel Comm
John Wiley & Sons

ProBlogger: Secrets for Blogging Your Way to a Six-Figure Income, 2nd Edition
Darren Rowse and Chris Garrett
Wiley

The Really, Really Easy Step-by-Step Guide To Building Your Own Website: For Absolute Beginers of All Ages
Gavin Hoole and Cheryl Smith
New Holland

Web Copy That Sells: The Revolutionary Formula for Creating Killer Copy That Grabs Their Attention and Compels Them to Buy, 2nd edition
Maria Veloso
AMACOM

**WordPress 24-Hour Trainer: Watch, Read and Learn How to Create and Customize WordPress Sites (Book and DVD)*
George Plumley
Wiley Publishing, Inc.

08 eBay Your Way to Mail Order Success

PayPal.com

Recommended Reading

eBay101: Selling on eBay for Part-time or Full-time Income, Beginner to Power Seller in 90 Days
Steve Weber
Weber Books

The Home-Based Bookstore: Start Your Own Business Selling Used Books on Amazon, eBay or Your Own Website
Steve Weber
Weber Books

09 No-Mail Mail Order

To Sell and Automatically Deliver E-books Online

Clickbank.com
Payloadz.com

Recommended Reading

Make Money Online: Write & Sell eBooks Guide
Scott Boyd
Globotic Media Publishing

---

* If you are interested in creating WordPress websites, this is the ultimate guide—highly recommended

10 The Mail Room

Packaging supplies

FTC.com

Packagingsupplies.com

USPS.com

Go to your post office for free Priority Mail packages

Mailing Fulfillment Service Association

1421 Prince St., Suite 410

Alexandria, VA 22314

(703) 836-9200

mfsanet.org

11 Growing Pains and Pleasures

Recommended Reading

Built To Sell: Turn Your Business Into One You Can Sell

John Warrillow

Flip Jet Media, Inc.

Conquer the Chaos: How to Grow a Successful Small Business Without Going Crazy

Clate Mask, Scott Martineau, and Michael E. Gerber

Wiley

Hiring Independent Contractors: The Employer's Legal Guide

Stephen Fishman and Amy Delpo

Nolo

Index

About the Author

Georganne Fiumara is a home business expert and consultant and the founder of Mothers' Home Business Network and their popular website, HomeWorkingMom.com. *Woman's World Magazine* has chosen Georganne as one of America's Ultimate Experts on earning money at home.

More than 100 of her articles on home business topics have appeared in national publications such as *Family Circle*, *Woman's Day*, *New Business Opportunities*, *Income Opportunities*, and *American Baby*, and she contributes to numerous websites. She is also the author of *Never Be Unemployed Again* and *How to Start a Home-Based Business to Become a Work-At-Home Mom* (Globe Pequot Press).